# Group IV Elements

© Inner London Education Authority 1984

First published 1984
by John Murray (Publishers) Ltd
50 Albemarle Street
London W1X 4BD

Printed and bound in Great Britain by
Martin's of Berwick

British Library Cataloguing in Publication Data

Independent Learning Project for Advanced
  Chemistry
  Group IV Elements. - (ILPAC;  Unit I4)
  1. Science
  I. Title       II. Series
  500            Q161.2

  ISBN 0 7195 4052 6

# CONTENTS

# PREFACE

This volume is one of twenty Units produced by ILPAC, the Independent Learning Project for Advanced Chemistry, written for students preparing for the Advanced Level examinations of the G.C.E. The Project has been sponsored by the Inner London Education Authority and the materials have been extensively tested in London schools and colleges. In its present revised form, however, it is intended for a wider audience; the syllabuses of all the major Examination Boards have been taken into account and questions set by these boards have been included.

Although ILPAC was initially conceived as a way of overcoming some of the difficulties presented by uneconomically small sixth forms, it has frequently been adopted because its approach to learning has certain advantages over more traditional teaching methods. Students assume a greater responsibility for their own learning and can work, to some extent, at their own pace, while teachers can devote more time to guiding individual students and to managing resources.

By providing personal guidance, and detailed solutions to the many exercises, supported by the optional use of video-cassettes, the Project allows students to study A-level chemistry with less teacher-contact time than a conventional course demands. The extent to which this is possible must be determined locally; potentially hazardous practical work must, of course, be supervised. Nevertheless, flexibility in time-tabling makes ILPAC an attractive proposition in situations where classes are small or suitably-qualified teachers are scarce.

In addition, ILPAC can provide at least a partial solution to other problems. Students with only limited access to laboratories, for example, those studying at evening classes, can concentrate upon ILPAC practical work in the laboratory, in the confidence that related theory can be systematically studied elsewhere. Teachers of A-level chemistry who are inexperienced, or whose main discipline is another science, will find ILPAC very supportive. The materials can be used effectively where upper and lower sixth form classes are timetabled together. ILPAC can provide 'remedial' material for students in higher education. Schools operating sixth form consortia can benefit from the cohesion that ILPAC can provide in a fragmented situation. The project can be adapted for use in parts of the world where there is a severe shortage of qualified chemistry teachers. And so on.

A more detailed introduction to ILPAC, with specific advice both to students and to teachers, is included in the first volume only. Details of the Project Team and Trial Schools appear inside the back cover.

LONDON 1983

# ACKNOWLEDGEMENTS

Thanks are due to the following examination boards for permission to reproduce questions from past A-level papers:

Joint Matriculation Board;

   Teacher-marked Exercises p45(1977), p57(1978)

Oxford Delegacy of Local Examinations;

   Level One Test 3(1981)

Southern Universities Joint Board;

   Exercise 22(1979)
   Level One Test 6(1980)
   End-of-Unit Test 11(1982), 12(1982)

University of London Entrance and School Examinations Council;

   Exercises 17(1980), 24(1973),
   Experiment 3 Q(1973), H and I(1980)
   Level One Test 1(1978)
   End-of-Unit Test 1(1983), 2(1977), 3(1976), 4-8(1981)
                    9(1978), 10(1978), 12(1982), 13(1974), 14(1977)

Where answers to these questions are included, they are provided by ILPAC and not by the examination boards.

Questions from papers of other examining boards appear in other Units.

The extract on pages 54 and 55 is reproduced by permission of Edward Arnold (Publishers) Ltd., from 'The Biochemistry of Pollution' by J.M. Ottaway.


Photographs are reproduced by permission as follows:

Telephone exchange equipment, p13 - British Telecom
Space shuttle, p13 - J. Allan Cash Photolibrary
Silicon compounds, p37 - Tony Langham
Siliconized rubber tubing, p37 - Stephen Devereux
Telephone cables, p38 - British Telecom
Galaxy, p45 - Popperfoto
Exhaust fumes, p53 - Tony Langham
Photographs of students - Tony Langham

# SYMBOLS USED IN ILPAC UNITS

 Reading

 Exercise

 Test

 'A' Level question

 'A' Level part question

 'A' Level question
Special paper

 Worked example

 Teacher-marked exercise

 Revealing exercises

 Discussion

 Computer programme

 Experiment

 Video programme

 Film loop

 Model-making

# INTERNATIONAL HAZARD SYMBOLS

 Harmful

 Toxic

 Radioactive

 Flammable

 Explosive

 Corrosive

 Oxidising

# INTRODUCTION

In this Unit we deal with the elements and compounds of Group IV, whose symbols we include in the outline Periodic Table below (Fig. 1).  We also briefly consider the position of hydrogen in the Periodic Table.

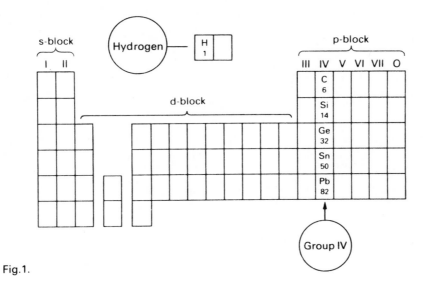

Fig.1.

In your study of Groups I, II and VII (the extreme groups of the Periodic Table), you learned that most of the gradations in properties are related to the increase of atomic size down each group, and that the anomaly of each top element is due to the very small size of its atoms.  These trends are also apparent in Group IV but the progressive change down a group is more noticeable with groups in the middle of the Periodic Table.  The most striking trend is the increase in metallic character: carbon and silicon are non-metals, germanium is a metalloid, while tin and lead are metals.  We focus our attention on this trend, and its implications, throughout this Unit.

As in Units I1 (The *s*-Block Elements), I2 (The Halogens) and I3 (The Periodic Table) we deal mainly with the physical and chemical properties of the elements in Level One and their compounds in Level Two.  In the appendix we consider some of the problems associated with lead pollution.

There are three experiments in this Unit, the last one being an 'observation and deduction' exercise.

'The Group IV elements' is an ILPAC videoprogramme designed to accompany this Unit.  Another, 'Carbon - the key to organic chemistry', may be useful; it includes some comparisons between carbon and silicon.  The programmes are not essential, but try to see them at the appropriate times if they are available.

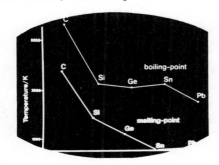

The Group IV elements

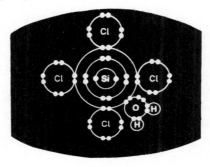

Carbon - the key to organic chemistry

# PRE-KNOWLEDGE

Before you start work on this Unit, you should be able to:

(1)   state the names and symbols of the elements in Group IV;

(2)   write the electron configurations of the elements in Group IV;

(3)   describe the appearance and structure of the two allotropes of carbon;

(4)   state the change in atomic radius, first ionization energy and metallic character within a group in the Periodic Table;

(5)   state the conditions under which carbon reacts with steam and name the products;

(6)   state the relative solubilities in water and acid-base nature of the following oxides and hydrides - $CO$, $CO_2$, $SiO_2$, $PbO$, $CH_4$ and $SiH_4$;

(7)   state the structure and bonding of the following oxides, hydrides and chlorides - $CO$, $CO_2$, $SiO_2$, $PbO$, $CH_4$, $SiH_4$, $CCl_4$ and $SiCl_4$.

(8)   state how lead(II) oxide may be reduced to lead;

(9)   name the series of silicon hydrides of general formula $Si_nH_{2n+2}$;

(10)   give an equation for the hydrolysis of silicon tetrachloride.


# PRE-TEST

To find out whether you are ready to start Level One, try the following test, which is based on the pre-knowledge items.  You should not spend more than 30 minutes on this test.  Hand your answers to your teacher for marking.

# PRE-TEST

1. (a) Complete a copy of Table 1, which is concerned with the electronic configuration of the Group IV elements.

   Table 1

   | Element | Atomic number | Full electronic structure | Outer shell only |
   |---------|---------------|---------------------------|------------------|
   | C | 6 | 2,4 | $2s^2 2p^2$ |
   | Si | 14 | | |
   | Ge | 32 | | |
   | Sn | 50 | | |
   | Pb | 82 | 2,8,18,32,18,4 | $6s^2 6p^2$ |

   (3)

   (b) Which elements in Group IV have only $s$ and $p$ electrons? (2)

2. The structures of the two allotropes of carbon are shown in Fig. 2.

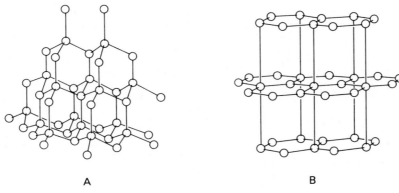

   A                                      B

   Fig.2.

   (a) Identify the two structures shown in Fig. 2. (1)

   (b) What name is given to the forces between the layers in B? (1)

   (c) Briefly describe each structure. (4)

   (d) Account for the following in terms of structure:

       (i) the hardness of diamond,

      (ii) the lubricating power of graphite,

     (iii) the electrical conductivity of graphite. (6)

3. What are the trends, as Group IV is descended, in the following:

   (a) atomic radius,

   (b) first ionization energy,

   (c) metallic character? (3)

3

4. Complete a copy of Table 2.

Table 2

| Formula of oxide | Solubility in water | Acid-base nature | Structural* type |
|---|---|---|---|
| CO | | | |
| $CO_2$ | | | |
| $SiO_2$ | | | |
| PbO | Insoluble | | |

*State whether the structure is simple molecular, giant molecular or giant ionic. (11)

5. (a) Copy and complete the equations shown below stating the conditions of each reaction.

    (i)   $C(s) + H_2O(g) \rightarrow$

    (ii)  $CO_2(g) + NaOH(aq) \rightarrow$

    (iii) $PbO(s) + C(s) \rightarrow$

    (iv) $CH_4(g) + O_2(g) \rightarrow$ (8)

  (b) What type of reaction is occurring in (a) (ii)? (1)

6. (a) Silicon forms a limited number of saturated hydrides. Give the name and general formula of this series. (2)

  (b) Draw the shape of the $SiH_4$ molecule. (2)

  (c) State the acid-base nature of $CH_4$ and $SiH_4$. (2)

7. Which of the following compounds is/are hydrolysed by water? Give equation(s) where necessary.

(a) $CH_4$    (b) $SiCl_4$    (c) $PbCl_2$    (d) $SiO_2$    (e) $CCl_4$ (4)

(Total 50 marks)

# LEVEL ONE

In Units I1 (*s*-Block Elements) and I2 (The Halogens) you learned that metallic character increases down Groups I, II and VII. From the appearance of the Group IV elements, situated in the middle of the Periodic Table, the change, with increasing atomic number, from non-metallic to metallic character is immediately striking.

This group also provides other examples of trends continuing and developing from one end of a group to the other. Thus, although every element bears a similarity to its immediate neighbours, the top and bottom elements, carbon and lead, have little in common.

To obtain a simple overall picture of Group IV, we suggest that you read the introduction to it in your text-book(s).

We begin this Unit in a similar way to Units I1 (*s*-Block Elements) and I2 (The Halogens) by considering the physical properties of these elements.


## PHYSICAL PROPERTIES

Objectives. When you have finished this section you should be able to:

(1) state the electronic configuration of the Group IV elements and their ions using the *s*, *p*, *d* notation;

(2) describe and explain the <u>changes in ionization energy</u> with increasing atomic number;

(3) explain the meaning of the term <u>'inert pair effect'</u>.

### Electron configuration

We start with this property because it influences the physical and chemical properties of the elements and their compounds.

Exercise 1   (a)   Write down the electron configuration of the following atoms and ions using the *s*, *p*, *d* notation:

       (i)   Sn and $Sn^{2+}$

       (ii)   Pb and $Pb^{2+}$

    (b)   Which outer-shell electrons are unaffected, so that they remain as part of the $Sn^{2+}$ and $Pb^{2+}$ ions?

    (c)   Which of the Group IV atom(s) do not contain *d* electrons?

    (d)   How many electrons could, in theory, occupy the outer shell of each of the atom(s) given in (c). Explain your answer.

    (Answers on page **58** )

Carbon and silicon have only *s*- and *p*-electrons but the other elements follow a completed transition series with ten *d*-electrons. This suggests that some differences can be expected between carbon and silicon and the rest of the group. Furthermore, silicon is capable of expanding its outer valence shell to accommodate 18 electrons while carbon is limited to 8 electrons. Thus, some differences are also expected between carbon and silicon.

We now look at ionization energies to see if these help us to explain why the outer *s*-electrons in tin and lead are not lost during ion formation and are therefore sometimes referred to as an 'inert pair'.

## Ionization energies

In the next exercise you look at the successive ionization energies for each element and explain the trend down the group in terms of atomic size.

Exercise 2   (a)   With the aid of your data book complete a copy of Table 3 below.

Table 3

| | Ionization energies/kJ mol$^{-1}$ | | | | |
|---|---|---|---|---|---|
| Element | 1st | 2nd | 3rd | 4th | 5th |
| C | | | | | |
| Si | | | | | |
| Ge | | | | | |
| Sn | | | | | |
| Pb | | | | | |

(b)   What is the trend in first ionization energy with increasing atomic number? Use the following graph (Fig. 3) to help you to explain the trend.

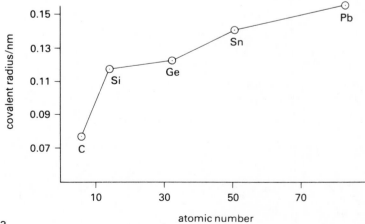

Fig.3.

6

(c) Do the successive (1st to 5th) ionization energies of the elements vary as you would expect? Explain your answer and comment on the jumps from the 4th to the 5th ionization energy.

(d) Plot a graph showing the difference between the 4th and 5th I.E. ($\Delta E$) for each element (vertical axis) against atomic number (horizontal axis). Explain the shape of your graph.

(Answers on page 58 )

As you have seen, all the ionization energies decrease sharply from carbon to silicon, but then change in an irregular way because of the effects of filling the $d$ and $f$ shells.

The jumps between the 4th and 5th ionization energies again suggest that carbon and silicon differ both from one another and from the rest of the group.

In the next exercise we look at the ionization energy data in a different way.

Exercise 3   The following graph (Fig. 4) shows the sums of the 1st and 2nd ionization energies, 3rd and 4th ionization energies and 1st, 2nd, 3rd and 4th ionization energies for each element. Study it and answer the questions which follow.

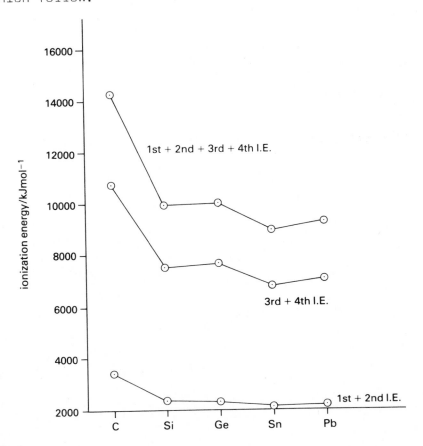

Fig.4.

Exercise 3
(continued)

(a) Which element differs markedly from the rest? Suggest a reason for your answer.

(b) Which element is least likely to form an $X^{4+}$ ion?

(c) Can you predict from the data which element is most likely to show non-metallic properties? Explain your answer.

(d) Can you predict from the data which two elements are most likely to be metals?

(e) Can you predict from the graph whether tin and lead are more likely to form divalent cations than are silicon and germanium?

(Answers on page 58 )

The ionization energy data do not suggest that the outer $s$-electrons take less part in bonding in the heavier elements of Group IV. If this were the case, we would expect a dramatic increase in the 3rd and 4th ionization energies on descending the group. This is not found. The jumps between the 2nd and 3rd ionization energies are similar to those between the 1st and 2nd ionization energies.

However, it is clear that the divalent state exists for tin and lead but not carbon and silicon. Although this was previously 'explained' in terms of the inert pair effect it is nowadays recognised that there is no easy way of explaining the relative stability of the +2 state for tin and lead. The phrase 'inert pair effect' is now used as a label for the phenomenon and means that the lower oxidation state becomes more stable as the group is descended. We shall return to this 'effect' when we consider the relative stabilities of the +4 and +2 oxidation states in the compounds of the Group IV elements.

Before we go on to compare other physical properties like melting-points and densities of the Group IV elements we must consider their structures.

# Structures and bonding of the Group IV elements

Objectives. When you have finished this section, you should be able to:

(4) state the structures and bonding found in the Group IV elements;

(5) describe the trend in density with increasing atomic number;

(6) relate the trend in density to the change in structure and bonding.

You should already be familiar with the structure and bonding of both graphite and diamond from Unit S4 (Bonding and Structure). Revise this if necessary and read about the structures of the other Group IV elements. Look for details of the allotropes of tin and a description of the change from non-metallic to metallic character with increasing atomic number in the group.

8

From what you have learned so far you may be under the impression that there are no similarities between the structures of diamond and graphite. The next exercise deals with similarities between the two structures.

Exercise 4   Fig. 5 shows a more unusual representation of the diamond structure. It is the same structure as that shown in Fig. 2 (in the pre-test) but drawn in a different way. Compare the diamond structure with the graphite structure and answer the questions which follow.

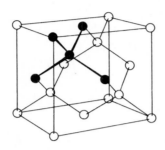

**Fig.5.   The unit cell of the diamond structure.**

(a)   What is the co-ordination number of each carbon atom in the two structures?

(b)   Describe any similarities which are apparent between the structures. (A model of the diamond structure will be helpful, if one is available.)

(Answers on page  58 )

You consider the structures of the other elements in the next exercise.

Exercise 5   (a)   Complete a larger copy of Table 4 using your data book as necessary.

Table 4

|   |   | Density/g cm$^{-3}$ | Structure | Bonding |
|---|---|---|---|---|
| C | Diamond | | | |
|   | Graphite | | | |
| Si | | | | |
| Ge | | | | |
| Sn | Grey (α) | | | |
|   | White (β) | | Tetragonal (Distorted close-packed) | |
| Pb | | | | |

9

Exercise 5    (b)  Describe the general trend in density with increasing
(continued)        atomic number.

             (c)  Describe the change in structure and bonding with increasing
                  atomic number.

             (d)  How does the general trend in density relate to the change
                  in structure and bonding?  Explain as far as possible.

             (e)  At which temperature is the grey allotrope of tin trans-
                  formed to the white form?

             (Answers on page 59 )


Structure and bonding are also closely related to other bulk physical
properties such as melting-point and boiling-point which we now consider.


Objective.  When you have finished this section, you should be able to:

(7)  describe the general trend in melting-points, boiling-points, heats of
     atomization and bond energies as the group is descended.


## Melting-points and boiling-points


In any comparison of properties like melting-point and boiling-point for the
Group IV elements we must consider their different structures.  With this in
mind attempt the next exercise.


Exercise 6    Study the graph below (Fig. 6) which shows the melting-
              points and boiling-points of the elements in Group IV,
              and answer the questions which follow.

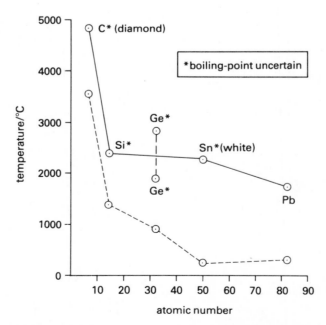

Fig.6.   Melting-points and boiling-points of the elements in Group IV

(a) Describe the trend in melting-points and boiling-points with increasing atomic number.

(b) What do the trends in (a) suggest about the cohesive forces between the atoms in each element?

(c) Approximate bond energies in Group IV elements are shown in Table 5.

Table 5   Comparison of bond energies/kJ mol$^{-1}$

| Bond | C — C | Si — Si | Ge — Ge | Sn — Sn |
|------|-------|---------|---------|---------|
| Energy | 356 | 210 - 250* | 190 - 210 | 105 - 145 |

*These values apply to the crystalline element and higher values are found for the Si — Si bond enthalpy in compounds of silicon.

Use these values to explain

(i) the large decrease in melting-point and boiling-point from carbon to silicon,

(ii) the steady decrease in melting-point between silicon and tin.

(d) How would you expect the enthalpies of atomization to change as the group is descended?

(e) The enthalpy of atomization of lead (195.8 kJ mol$^{-1}$) is less than that of tin (white) (301.2 kJ mol$^{-1}$) but the melting-point of lead is greater than that of tin (white). Suggest a reason for this.

(Answers on page 59 )

You now consider the structures of these elements in relation to some of their other physical properties, such as electrical conductivity, hardness and electronegativity.


# Other important physical properties


Objectives.   When you have finished this section you should be able to:

(8) state the trends in electrical conductivity, hardness and electro-negativity with increasing atomic number;

(9) describe uses of the elements based on their physical properties.


When the periodic classification was first suggested, germanium was not known.  However, Mendéleev was so certain of the fundamental nature of group trends that, in 1871, he predicted the discovery of a new element, which he called 'eka-silicon'.  He also predicted its properties, based on those of the Group IV elements, and these predictions were srikingly confirmed when germanium was eventually discovered in 1886.

The element germanium, whose properties
were predicted accurately by Mendeléev.

Tabelle II.

| Gruppe III. — R²O³ | Gruppe IV. RH⁴ RO² | Gruppe V. RH³ R²O⁵ | Gruppe VI. RH² RO³ |
|---|---|---|---|
| = 11 | C = 12 | N = 14 | O = 16 |
| Al = 27,3 | Si = 28 | P = 31 | S = 3 |
| − = 44 | Ti = 48 | V = 51 | Cr = 52 |
| − = 68 | − = 72 | As = 75 | Se = 7 |
| Yt = 88 | Zr = 90 | Nb = 94 | Mo = 96 |
| In = 113 | Sn = 118 | Sb = 122 | Te = 1 |

A copy of part of Mendeléev's original
Periodic Table showing the gap (circled)
later to be filled by germanium.

In the next exercise you also make certain predictions about selected
elements in this group using your knowledge so far.

Exercise 7   (a)   Complete a larger copy of Table 6 using your
knowledge of the structures of the elements, and of
the trends you expect to encounter as the group is
descended.

Table 6

| | | Electrical conductivity | Hardness and malleability |
|---|---|---|---|
| C | Graphite | | |
| | Diamond | | |
| Si | | Semi-conductor | Hard and brittle |
| Ge | | | |
| Sn | Grey (α) | Semi-conductor | Hard and brittle |
| | White (β) | | |
| Pb | | | |

(b)   Which element is likely to be the most electronegative?

(c)   Which element is likely to be the least electronegative?

(Answers on page 59 )

The next exercise is concerned with the uses of the Group IV elements, based
on their physical properties.

Exercise 8 Complete a larger copy of Table 7.

Table 7

| Element | | Uses of element | Physical property employed |
|---|---|---|---|
| C | Diamond | Gemstones<br>Cutting tools<br>Abrasives | |
| | Graphite | Lubricants<br>Pencils<br>Electrodes | |
| Si | | Transistors<br>Computers<br>Rectifiers | Semi-conductivity |
| Ge | | Transistors<br>Rectifiers | |
| Sn (white) | | Tin-plating steel<br>Solders (alloys<br>of Sn, Pb and Sb) | |
| Pb | | Car batteries | Electrical conductivity (and chemical properties) |
| | | Radiation shields<br>Roofing<br>Solders | High density |

(Answers on page 60 )

Silicon and germanium are used to make the chips in microprocessor-controlled telephone exchanges.

Graphite (a poor conductor of heat) is used on the leading edges of the wings of the space-shuttle.

All the physical properties considered so far point to the most striking feature of the group, i.e. the increase in metallic character with increasing atomic number.  This trend is also reflected in the chemical properties of the elements, which we now briefly consider.

# CHEMICAL PROPERTIES

The elements as a whole are not very reactive, but trends are evident as the group is descended.  We deal with their chemical properties very briefly in this section and we also look at selected reactions of the aqueous divalent ions of tin and lead.  Most of the work on the compounds of the Group IV elements is covered in Level Two.

Objectives.  When you have finished this section, you should be able to:

(10)    describe the reactions of the Group IV elements with oxygen, chlorine, water, alkalis and acids;

(11)    illustrate the gradual change from non-metallic to metallic character with increasing atomic number in Group IV by reference to the chemical properties of the elements;

(12)    state the trends in stability of the +4 and +2 oxidation states of the Group IV elements in their compounds;

(13)    write equations for the reactions of the divalent aqueous ions of tin and lead with solutions of sodium hydroxide and ammonia;

(14)    give examples of reactions in which aqueous divalent tin ions behave as reducing agents;

(15)    describe the reactions of divalent aqueous lead ions with hydrochloric acid and potassium chromate solution.

You start this section with an experiment on the reactions of tin and lead and their divalent aqueous ions.

# EXPERIMENT 1

The reactions of tin and lead
and their aqueous ions

## Aim

The purpose of this experiment is two-fold: to
show the reactions of tin and lead with acids
and to familiarise you with some of the common
reactions of $Pb^{2+}$(aq) and $Sn^{2+}$(aq).

## Introduction

In this experiment you find out if the metallic character of tin and lead
is evident from their reactions with acids.  You treat the elements with two
acids; an oxidizing agent (nitric acid) and a non-oxidizing acid (hydrochloric acid).  In each case you attempt to identify any gases evolved.

The reactions of the divalent ions are included here to demonstrate the
relative stability of the +2 state in tin and lead.

## Requirements

safety spectacles
15 test-tubes
2 test-tube racks
test-tube holder
Bunsen burner and mat
lead (small pieces)
hydrochloric acid, dilute, 2 M HCl
hydrochloric acid, concentrated, HCl – – – – – – – – – – – – – – – – – – – – –
3 teat pipettes
beaker, 250 cm³
wood splints
universal indicator paper
nitric acid, concentrated, $HNO_3$ – – – – – – – – – – – – – – – – – – –
tin (small pieces)
sticky labels for test-tubes
0.1 M solution of $Sn^{2+}$ ions (in dilute hydrochloric acid)
0.1 M solution of $Pb^{2+}$ ions – – – – – – – – – – – – – – – – – – – – –
sodium hydroxide solution, 2 M NaOH
ammonia solution, 2 M $NH_3$
potassium manganate(VII) solution, 0.01 M $KMnO_4$ (in dilute ethanoic acid)
potassium chromate(VI) solution, 0.1 M $K_2CrO_4$
sodium sulphide solution, 0.02 M $Na_2S$ – – – – – – – – – – – – –
potassium iodide solution, 0.1 M KI

<table>
<tr><td>Hazard warning</td><td></td></tr>
</table>

Hazard warning

Lead compounds are harmful if ingested or absorbed through the skin.

Sodium sulphide is toxic and corrosive and evolves highly poisonous hydrogen sulphide gas on contact with acids.

Concentrated hydrochloric acid is very corrosive.

Concentrated nitric acid is very corrosive and a powerful oxidant.

Therefore you MUST:

WEAR PROTECTIVE GLOVES AND SAFETY SPECTACLES.

USE SODIUM SULPHIDE IN THE FUME-CUPBOARD.

Procedure

1. Place a small piece of lead in each of 3 test-tubes.

2. To one test-tube add about 2 cm³ of dilute hydrochloric acid and heat gently. Can you see or detect a gas? If not, repeat the experiment carefully using about 2 cm³ of concentrated hydrochloric acid.

3. In the remaining test-tube add about 2 cm³ of concentrated nitric acid to the lead and heat gently.

4. Place a small piece of tin in each of two test-tubes and repeat steps 2 and 3.

5. Record your results in a larger copy of Results Table 1.

6. Add approximately 2 cm³ of the Sn²⁺ solution to each of seven test-tubes.

7. Add approximately 2 cm³ of the Pb²⁺ solution to each of seven test-tubes.

8. Add each of the following reagents to separate portions of the Sn²⁺ and Pb²⁺ solutions:

   (a) dilute sodium hydroxide solution, initially drop-by-drop, and then to excess;

   (b) ammonia solution, initially drop-by-drop, and then to excess;

   (c) about 2 cm³ of dilute hydrochloric acid, heat the mixtures and then cool them under running cold water;

   (d) about 2 cm³ of acidified potassium manganate(VII) solution;

   (e) about 1 cm³ of potassium chromate(VI) solution;

   (f) 5 drops of sodium sulphide solution (do this in the fume-cupboard and dispose of the mixture by pouring into the fume-cupboard sink);

   (g) about 2 cm³ of aqueous potassium iodide.

9. Record your observations in a larger copy of Results Table 2.

Results Table 1

| Acid | Tin | Lead |
|---|---|---|
| Dilute hydrochloric acid | | |
| Concentrated hydrochloric acid | | |
| Concentrated nitric acid | | |

(Specimen results on page **61** )

Results Table 2

| Reagent | $Sn^{2+}(aq)$(acidified) | $Pb^{2+}(aq)$ |
|---|---|---|
| (a) Sodium hydroxide solution | | |
| (b) Ammonia solution | | |
| (c) Dilute hydrochloric acid | | |
| (d) Acidified potassium manganate(VII) solution | | |
| (e) Potassium chromate(VI) solution | | |
| (f) Sodium sulphide solution | | |
| (g) Potassium iodide solution | | |

(Specimen results on page **61** )

Questions

1.  (a)  Complete the following equations:

$$Pb(s) + HCl(aq) \rightarrow$$

$$Sn(s) + HCl(aq) \rightarrow$$

2.  Are the reactions between the elements and hydrochloric acid typical of metals?  Explain your answer.

3.  Reactions with nitric acid tend to be complex and equations are not generally required.  The questions illustrate some general points.

    (a)  Which gas did you detect when nitric acid reacted with tin and lead?

    (b)  Do other metals behave in a similar way with nitric acid?  Give one example.

(c) Why does nitric acid behave differently from hydrochloric acid?

4. Use your text-book(s) to complete and balance the equations in (a larger copy of) Table 8. In the comments column you should describe the type of chemical reaction occurring and any other important feature(s).

Table 8

| Equations | Comments |
|---|---|
| $Sn^{2+}(aq) + OH^-(aq) \rightarrow$ <br><br> $Sn(OH)_2(s) + OH^-(aq) \rightarrow$ | The precipitate dissolves in excess NaOH to form a stannate(II) ion*, $Sn(OH)_6^{4-}$. |
| $Pb^{2+}(aq) + OH^-(aq) \rightarrow$ <br><br> $Pb(OH)_2(s) + OH^-(aq) \rightarrow$ | |
| $2MnO_4^-(aq) + 16H^+(aq) + 5Sn^{2+}(aq) \rightarrow$ | |
| $Pb^{2+}(aq) + 2Cl^-(aq) \rightarrow$ | Simple precipitation reaction. Precipitate soluble in hot water. |
| $Cr_2O_7^{2-}(aq)** + H^+(aq) + Sn^{2+}(aq) \rightarrow$ | |
| $Pb^{2+}(aq) + CrO_4^{2-}(aq) \rightarrow$ | |
| $Pb^{2+}(aq) + S^{2-}(aq) \rightarrow$ | |
| $Sn^{2+}(aq) + S^{2-}(aq) \rightarrow$ | |
| $Pb^{2+}(aq) + I^-(aq) \rightarrow$ | |

*Various formulae have been proposed for the stannate(II) ion ranging from $SnO_2^{2-}$ for the anhydrous form to $Sn(OH)_4^{2-}$ and $Sn(OH)_6^{4-}$ for the hydrated forms. $Sn(OH)_6^{4-}$ seems the most probable. Similar variations have been proposed for the plumbate(II) ion $Pb(OH)_6^{4-}$.

**Chromate(VI) $(CrO_4^{2-})$ changes to dichromate(VI) $(Cr_2O_7^{2-})$ when acidified $(2CrO_4^{2-}(aq) + 2H^+(aq) \rightleftharpoons Cr_2O_7^{2-}(aq) + H_2O(l))$

5. In the experiment, potassium manganate(VII) solution was acidified with dilute ethanoic acid and not, as is usual, dilute hydrochloric acid or dilute sulphuric acid. With the aid of your text-book(s), explain why you think this change was made. Give any relevant equations in your answer and state what you would observe if the $MnO_4^-$ solution were acidified with HCl(aq) or $H_2SO_4$(aq).

6. State which of the divalent ions ($Sn^{2+}$ and $Pb^{2+}$) is more stable. Explain your answer.

7. Predict the reaction between aqueous tin(II) ions and a solution of mercury(II) chloride. What do you think you would observe in this reaction?

(Answers on page 61 )

You may have been surprised at the unreactive nature of lead compared to tin in its reactions with acids. This is also surprising in view of the fact that lead and tin are very close to each other in the electrochemical series. The reactivity of lead is to some extent suppressed by its tendency to form insoluble coatings of, for example, an oxide, chloride or sulphate.

Now you study some further chemical properties of Group IV elements.

By reference to your text-book(s) find out about the reactions of the elements in Group IV with reagents such as <u>oxygen</u>, <u>chlorine</u>, <u>water</u>, <u>alkalis</u> and <u>concentrated hydrochloric acid</u>. Use Table 9 below as a guide in your reading, so that you can complete it in the next exercise.

Table 9

| Reagent | General Reaction | Comments | | | | |
|---|---|---|---|---|---|---|
| | | Carbon | Silicon | Germanium | Tin | Lead |
| Oxygen | $X + O_2 \rightarrow XO_2$<br>Except Pb ($\rightarrow$ PbO). | | Burns at red heat. | Slow at red heat. | Slow at white heat. | |
| Chlorine | $X + 2Cl_2 \rightarrow XCl_4$<br>Except Pb ($\rightarrow$ PbCl$_2$). | | | | $SnCl_4$ on heating. | |
| Water | $X + 2H_2O \rightarrow XO_2 + 2H_2$<br>Except C ($\rightarrow$ CO) and Pb ($\rightarrow$ moderately soluble Pb(OH)$_2$ in aerated soft water, <u>PbSO$_4$(s)</u> in hard). | | Hot Si + steam react | Very hot Ge and steam react slightly, if at all. | | |
| Alkalis | $H_2$ and oxo-anion* salts formed | No reaction. | Hot conc. alkali needed. | Hot conc. alkali needed. | Slow in hot conc. alkali. | Molten alkali needed. |
| Conc. hydro-chloric acid | $X + 2H^+ \rightarrow X^{2+} + H_2$ | No reaction. | No reaction. | No reaction. | | |

*Silicate(IV), germanate(IV), mainly stannate(II) and plumbate(II) salts formed as appropriate.

Exercise 9 (a) Complete a larger copy of Table 9 on the previous page.

(b) With reference to the compounds formed in (a) answer the following questions:

(i) What is the common oxidation state of lead in its compounds?

(ii) What are the common oxidation states of the other Group IV elements?

(c) Do the reactions in (a) demonstrate the change from non-metallic to metallic character as Group IV is descended? Explain your answer.

(d) Why do you think the use of lead pipes is particularly undesirable for the supply of drinking-water in soft water areas?

(Answers on page 60 )

We briefly consider the topic of lead pollution in the appendix to this Unit.

It is evident from the previous exercise and experiment that the +2 oxidation state becomes more stable and the +4 oxidation state more unstable as the group is descended. Fig. 7 qualitatively summarises the relative stabilities of these two oxidation states for the elements in Group IV.

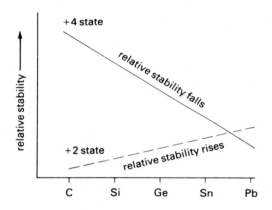

Fig.7 Relative stabilities of the +2 and +4 oxidation states for the elements in Group IV.

Use Fig. 7 to answer the next exercise.

Exercise 10 (a) Which is the more stable oxidation state of tin?

(b) Would you expect compounds of:

(i) silicon to exist in the +2 oxidation state,

(ii) lead to exist in the +4 oxidation state?

Explain your answers.

(c) The stability of +2 oxidation state increases with increasing atomic number. What label is attached to this phenomenon?

(Answers on page 62 )

# LEVEL ONE CHECKLIST

You have now reached the end of Level One of this Unit. The following is a summary of the objectives in Level One. Read carefully through them and check that you have adequate notes. At this stage, you should be able to:

(1) state the electronic configurations of the Group IV elements and their ions using the $s$, $p$, $d$ notation;

(2) describe and explain the changes in ionization energy with increasing atomic number;

(3) explain the meaning of the term 'inert pair effect';

(4) state the structures and bonding found in the Group IV elements;

(5) describe the trend in density with increasing atomic number;

(6) relate the trend in density to the change in structure and bonding;

(7) describe the general trend in melting-points, boiling-points, heats of atomization and bond energies as the group is descended;

(8) state the trends in electrical conductivity, hardness and electro-negativity with increasing atomic number;

(9) describe uses of the elements based on their physical properties;

(10) describe the reactions of the Group IV elements with oxygen, chlorine, water, alkalis and acids;

(11) use the chemical properties of the Group IV elements to illustrate the gradual change from non-metallic to metallic character with increasing atomic number;

(12) state the trends in stability of the +4 and +2 oxidation states of the Group IV elements in their compounds;

(13) write equations for the reactions of the divalent aqueous ions of tin and lead with solutions of sodium hydroxide and ammonia;

(14) give examples of reactions in which aqueous divalent tin ions behave as reducing agents;

(15) describe the reactions of divalent aqueous lead ions with hydrochloric acid and potassium chromate solution.

# LEVEL ONE TEST

To find out how well you have learned the material in Level One, try the test which follows. Read the notes below before starting.

1. You should spend about 1 hour on this test.

2. Hand your answer to your teacher for marking.

# LEVEL ONE TEST

1. The elements in Group IV of the Periodic Table (*p*-block) are, in increasing order of atomic number, C, Si, Ge, Sn, Pb.

   (a) (i) What is the common feature of the electronic structure of these elements?

   (ii) Write down the full electronic configuration (*s*,*p*,*d*) of Sn (atomic number 50). (2)

   (b) Sn, and to a greater extent, Pb, are said to show the <u>inert pair</u> effect.

   (i) What is meant by the <u>inert pair</u> effect?

   (ii) Give ONE reason or piece of evidence which supports the existence of this effect. (3)

   (c) The diagram shows a plot of melting-point against atomic number for the elements in Group IV.

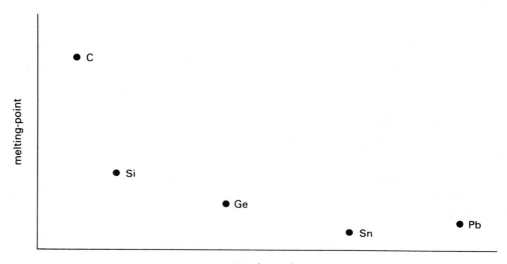

   **Fig.8.**

   (i) Why is the melting-point of carbon so much higher than that of the others?

   (ii) Suggest a reason for the steady fall in melting-point from Si to Sn. (4)

2. How do the following properties vary from carbon to lead?

   (a) The crystal structure of the elements. (4)

   (b) The element-element bond energies. (1)

   (c) The enthalpies of atomization. (1)

   Suggest explanations for (b) and (c). (4)

3. The first six ionization energies of an element A are given below:

| 1st | 2nd | 3rd | 4th | 5th | 6th |
|-----|-----|-----|-----|-----|-----|
| 787 | 1577 | 3230 | 4355 | 16090 | 19795 kJ mol$^{-1}$ |

A part

(a) To what group of the Periodic Table does A belong and why? (1)

(b) What is the formula of the highest chloride formed by A? (1)

4. (a) How, and under what conditions, do the elements tin and lead react with the following:

   (i) chlorine,   (ii) hydrochloric acid? (6)

   (b) How would you distinguish between aqueous solutions of $Pb^{2+}$ and $Sn^{2+}$ ions? (2)

5. Suggest an explanation for the following statement:

   In a particularly severe winter, organ pipes in a church in St Petersburg (made of an alloy rich in tin) are said to have crumbled. (2)

6. (a) Explain what happens when:

A part

   (i) aqueous solutions of tin(II) chloride and mercury(II) chloride are mixed; (5)

   (ii) hydrogen sulphide is passed through an aqueous solution of tin(II) chloride; (4)

   (iii) sodium hydroxide solution is added to an aqueous solution of tin(II) chloride until the alkali is in excess. (7)

   (b) Arrange the +2 oxidation states of germanium, lead, and tin in order of increasing ease of oxidation. Explain your answer. (3)

(Total 50 marks)

# LEVEL TWO

## COMPOUNDS OF GROUP IV ELEMENTS

In this section we consider three important groups of compounds formed by
the Group IV elements: the hydrides, oxides and chlorides.  Before you study
them in detail it will be helpful to look at some of their general features.


## General features of the compounds

You have already met most of the points we are about to make.  They are
central themes in the study of the Group IV compounds and you should look
out for examples which illustrate them as you progress through Level Two.

1.  The compounds further reflect:

    (a)  the change from non-metallic to metallic character going down the
         group;

    (b)  the unique nature of carbon;

    (c)  the steady increase in the stability of the +2 oxidation state
         relative to the +4 oxidation state with increasing atomic number
         of the Group IV elements.

2.  Most of the +4 compounds are essentially covalent.

3.  The +2 compounds tend to be more ionic.

With these points in mind, we start with the hydrides.


## Hydrides of Group IV elements

You have already studied some  of the hydrides of carbon and silicon in
Unit I3 (The Periodic Table).  If you have also studied Unit 01 (Hydro-
carbons) you will be familiar with some of the many other hydrides of carbon.
Here you extend your knowledge to include the other members of Group IV.


<u>Objectives.</u>  When you have finished this section, you should be able to:

(16)  explain why <u>carbon</u> forms an <u>enormous number of hydrides</u>;

(17)  explain the meaning of the term <u>catenation</u>;

(18)  state the <u>range of hydrides</u> formed by Si, Ge, Sn and Pb.


To give yourself an overview of the unique properties of carbon you
should watch the ILPAC video-programme 'Carbon, the key to organic
chemistry', if it is available.  You might have seen this video-tape
if you have already studied Unit 01 (Hydrocarbons).

Read about the hydrides of the Group IV elements looking for information about their stability, the range of hydrides formed by each element and the meaning of the term catenation.

Now try the following exercise which is concerned with the range of hydrides formed by each element in Group IV.

Exercise 11  Carbon forms an enormous range of singly bonded hydrides, the alkanes, which you study in Unit 01 (Hydrocarbons).

    (a)  Describe the extent of hydride formation for the other elements in Group IV.

    (b)  Explain the meaning of the term 'catenation'.

    (c)  Is the bonding in the other Group IV hydrides similar to that in the alkanes?

    (d)  Describe the structure of the Group IV tetrahydrides.

    (Answers on page 62 )

Carbon's ability to catenate to such a great extent can be related to bond energies.  Table 10 lists various bond energies involving Group IV elements. Study the table and attempt the exercise which follows.

Table 10  Bond energies of Group IV elements $(X)$/kJ mol$^{-1}$

| Bond | C | Si | Ge | Sn |
|------|-----|---------|---------|---------|
| X-X | 356 | 210-250 | 190-210 | 105-145 |
| X-H | 414 | 318 | 285 | 251 |
| X-O | 360 | 464 | 360 | —— |

We have omitted values for lead because lead atoms show little tendency to bond with each other.

Exercise 12  (a)  Which element forms the strongest bonds with itself (X-X)?

    (b)  Which element forms the strongest bonds with hydrogen (X-H)?

    (c)  For which element is $E$(X-H) closest to $E$(X-X)?

    (d)  Which element bonds more strongly to hydrogen than it does to oxygen?

    (e)  Which Group IV element has the least readily oxidized hydrides?

    (Answers on page 62 )

For catenation to occur an element must have a valency of at least two and be able to form strong bonds with itself. These bonds must also be of about the same strength as those in other elements such as oxygen and hydrogen (i.e. X-O and X-H). Stronger (or approximately equal) X-X bonds compared to X-O bonds make oxidation or hydrolysis of the catenated hydrides less energetically feasible. It is therefore not surprising that catenated compounds of carbon are the only ones formed naturally. However, catenated hydrides of the other Group IV elements have been synthesized by chemists.

Now attempt the next exercise which is concerned with multiple bond formation between Group IV elements in their hydrides.

Exercise 13   In addition to the alkanes carbon forms other series of hydrides such as the alkenes and alkynes.

    (a)   What are the structural characteristics of these hydrides?

    (b)   Do the other Group IV elements form hydrides corresponding to the alkenes and alkynes?

    (Answers on page 62 )

It has been suggested that multiple bond formation in the hydrides occurs only for carbon because good overlap of the relevant orbitals (e.g. $sp^2$ hybrid orbitals and $p$ orbitals in the formation of ethene) is only possible for carbon (since carbon contains the smallest atoms of Group IV). Thus σ and π bonds tend to be formed together in the hydrides of carbon but not in the hydrides of the other elements. However, reservations have been expressed about this idea and you need not trouble yourself for an explanation.

We now look at the thermal dissociation and general reactivity of the Group IV hydrides and see how these relate to the decreasing stability of the tetravalent state with increasing atomic number.

# Thermal dissociation and reactivity of the hydrides

Objective.   When you have finished this section you should be able to:

(19)   state the trend in (a) thermal dissociation and (b) reactivity of the tetrahydrides down the group.

When the tetrahydrides are heated in the absence of air they dissociate into their elements as shown by the following general equation:

      $XH_4 \rightarrow X + 2H_2$ (where X = Group IV element)

Fig. 9 shows the temperature at which Group IV hydrides dissociate.  Study the diagram and then answer the exercise which follows.

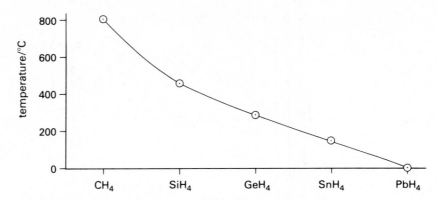

Fig.9.   The thermal dissociation of the tetrahydrides of Group IV.

Exercise 14   (a)   Describe the trend in thermal stability of Group IV hydrides.

(b)   Is this the trend you would expect from your knowledge of the stability of the Group IV compounds in the tetravalent state?

(Answers on page 62 )


In the next exercise you make predictions about the relative reactivities of the hydrides.


Exercise 15   (a)   From what you have learned so far about the Group IV hydrides, predict the order of reactivity on descending the group.

(b)   Methane, $CH_4$, is stable in air until ignited, but all the other tetrahydrides are spontaneously flammable.  Write an equation for the reaction between silane, $SiH_4$, and oxygen based on your knowledge of the reaction between methane and oxygen.

(Answers on page 62 )


Next, we consider the oxides of the elements in Group IV.

# Oxides of Group IV elements

In this section we consider the range of oxides formed by the elements, their methods of preparation, acid-base nature, structure and bonding.

Objectives.  When you have finished this section, you should be able to:

(20)   describe the preparation of tin(IV) oxide and lead(IV) oxide;

(21)   describe briefly the preparation of the oxides of the remaining elements in this Group in the +4 oxidation state;

(22)   state the appearance, acid-base nature, structure and bonding of the oxides;

(23)   give examples to illustrate the relative stabilities of the oxides in the +4 and +2 oxidation states.

In the next experiment you prepare tin(IV) oxide and lead(IV) oxide and compare their reactions.

## EXPERIMENT 2

The preparations and reactions of tin(IV) oxide and lead(IV) oxide

Aim

The purpose of this experiment is to prepare tin(IV) oxide and lead(IV) oxide and compare their reactions and relative stabilities.

Introduction

In parts A and B of this experiment you react tin and lead with concentrated nitric acid.  However, although this acid oxidizes tin to tin(IV) oxide, it oxidizes lead only to the +2 state.  In order to reach the +4 state, you add a stronger oxidizing agent to the lead(II) compound (e.g. sodium chlorate(I) solution (sodium hypochlorite) in alkaline solution) to form lead(IV) oxide.

Since the preparation of lead(IV) oxide involves more than one stage we ask you to calculate the percentage yield in order to test the efficiency of the method and your practical techniques.

In part C of this experiment you compare the effect of heat on tin(IV) oxide and lead(IV) oxide and the effect of various reagents on these two oxides.

## Requirements

safety spectacles
access to fume-cupboard
access to balance
disposable gloves
granulated tin
evaporating basin
Bunsen burner, tripod and gauze
measuring cylinder, 10 cm³
measuring cylinder, 100 cm³
nitric acid, concentrated, $HNO_3$ — — — — — — — — — — — — — — — —
3 teat pipettes
glass rod
spatula
suction filtration apparatus
distilled water
2 specimen tubes
sticky labels
lead foil
conical flask, 250 cm³
sodium hydroxide solution, 2 M NaOH — — — — — — — — — — — —
sodium chlorate(I) solution (hypochlorite), 1.5 M NaClO — — — — — — — —
nitric acid, 2 M $HNO_3$
propanone, $CH_3COCH_3$ — — — — — — — — — — — — — — — — —
tin(IV) oxide, $SnO_2$
lead(IV) oxide, $PbO_2$
10 test-tubes
test-tube holder
splints
hydrochloric acid, dilute, 2 M HCl
hydrochloric acid, concentrated, HCl — — — — — — — — — — — — — —
blue litmus paper
sodium hydroxide solution, 8 M NaOH — — — — — — — — — — — —
potassium iodide solution (acidified), 2 M KI

---

### Hazard warning

Concentrated hydrochloric acid, nitric acid and sodium hydroxide are very corrosive.  The vapours of the concentrated acids are also harmful to eyes, lung and skin.  Concentrated nitric acid is an oxidizing agent.  Therefore you MUST:

WEAR SAFETY SPECTACLES

AVOID CONTACT WITH SKIN

USE THESE SUBSTANCES IN THE FUME-CUPBOARD

Nitrogen dioxide and chlorine are toxic.  Therefore you MUST:

USE A FUME-CUPBOARD WHEN THESE GASES ARE GENERATED.

Propanone is very flammable.  Therefore you MUST:

KEEP THE STOPPER ON THE BOTTLE AS MUCH AS POSSIBLE
AND KEEP THE LIQUID AWAY FROM FLAMES.

Procedure

## A.  Preparation of tin(IV) oxide

1.  Weigh about 1.5 g of granulated tin and place it in an evaporating basin in the fume cupboard.

2.  Carefully pour 5 cm³ of concentrated nitric acid over the tin. Warm the mixture, if necessary, until the reaction is proceeding moderately.

3.  As the evolution of gas subsides stir the contents of the basin carefully with a glass rod.

4.  When the reaction appears to be complete add a few drops of concentrated nitric acid and warm carefully.  If brown fumes are evolved, the reaction is not complete, in which case add a few more drops of concentrated nitric acid and warm until the brown fumes cease.

5.  When cool, transfer the contents of the basin (mainly solid) to the suction filtration apparatus.

6.  Wash the precipitate thoroughly with distilled water until there is no sign of a yellow colouration.

7.  Transfer the precipitate (hydrated tin(IV) oxide) to an evaporating basin and heat (gently to start with, in order to avoid 'spitting', and then strongly).

8.  When cool, record the appearance of the solid in a copy of Results Table 3 and transfer the solid to a labelled specimen bottle.

## B.  Preparation of lead(IV) oxide

1.  Weigh about 5 g of lead (small pieces of foil), record the mass, and place it in a conical flask.

2.  Pour 10 cm³ of distilled water into the flask followed by 10 cm³ of concentrated nitric acid.

3.  Heat the flask gently in the fume cupboard until the reaction proceeds at a moderate rate.

4.  Gradually add about 5-10 cm³ of distilled water to replace any water lost by evaporation.

5.  When all the lead has reacted allow the mixture to cool to room temperature.

6.  If crystals (of lead(II) nitrate) appear on cooling add a little distilled water to dissolve them.

7.  Add dilute sodium hydroxide with a teat pipette and swirl the contents until a permanent faint white precipitate appears.

8.  Pour in a further 50 cm³ of sodium hydroxide solution followed by 30 cm³ of sodium chlorate(I) solution (sodium hypochlorite) and carefully bring the contents of the flask to the boil.

9.  Allow the precipitate to settle and carefully pour off the clear liquid.

10.  Add 100 cm³ of distilled water, shake and again pour off the clear liquid.

11.  Add 20 cm³ of dilute nitric acid followed by 50 cm³ of distilled water and shake again.

12.  Filter the precipitate at the pump and wash thoroughly with distilled water, followed by two 5 cm³ portions of propanone.

13. Draw air through the solid for about 5-10 minutes to allow the propanone to evaporate.

14. Leave the solid in a warm place for a day or two and, when you are satisfied that it is completely dry, weigh it.

15. Record your results in a copy of Results Table 3 and calculate the percentage yield based on the lead used.

## C. Reactions of tin(IV) oxide and lead(IV) oxide

Carry out the following tests on separate samples of the oxides which you have already prepared, and record your results in a larger copy of Results Table 4. We suggest that you also use tin(IV) oxide prepared by the manufacturers for the tests with the concentrated acids and alkalis since the oxide prepared by the above method is particularly insoluble.

1. Heat a spatula-ful of each oxide separately in a test-tube. Identify any gases given off.

2. To half a spatula measure of each oxide (approximately 0.1 g) add about 1 $cm^3$ of dilute hydrochloric acid in the fume cupboard. Identify any gas given off.

3. (a) Add approximately 0.1 g of lead(IV) oxide to 1 $cm^3$ of concentrated hydrochloric acid in the fume cupboard, identify the gas evolved and note the colour of the final solution.

   (b) Add half a spatula-tip (or less) of tin(IV) oxide to 1 $cm^3$ of concentrated hydrochloric acid and very cautiously warm the mixture in the fume cupboard. Does any of the solid dissolve?

   (c) Add half a spatula-tip (or less) of each oxide separately to 1 $cm^3$ of concentrated sodium hydroxide (8 M NaOH) and very cautiously warm the mixture in the fume cupboard.

   (d) Add approximately 0.1 g of each oxide separately to 2 $cm^3$ of acidified KI solution.

Results Table 3

| Mass of Pb | |
|---|---|
| Mass of $PbO_2$ | |
| % yield | |
| Appearance of $PbO_2$ | |
| Appearance of $SnO_2$ | |

(Specimen results on page 62 )

Results Table 4

| Test | Tin(IV) oxide | Lead(IV) oxide |
|---|---|---|
| (a) Heat | | |
| (b) Dilute hydrochloric acid | | |
| (c) Concentrated hydrochloric acid | | |
| (d) Concentrated sodium hydroxide | | |
| (e) Acidified potassium iodide | | |

(Specimen results on page 63 )


Questions

1.  Write an equation for the effect of heat on lead(IV) oxide.

2.  What is happening in the reactions between (a) lead(IV) oxide and dilute hydrochloric acid and (b) lead(IV) oxide and acidified potassium iodide?

3.  Find out from your text-book(s) the identity of the yellow liquid formed when lead(IV) oxide reacts with concentrated hydrochloric acid.

4.  Write equations for the reactions between (a) tin(IV) oxide and concentrated sodium hydroxide and (b) lead(IV) oxide and concentrated sodium hydroxide.

5.  What is the acid-base nature of tin(IV) oxide and lead(IV) oxide? (Bear in mind that concentrated sulphuric acid will attack tin(IV) oxide to form tin(IV) sulphate.)

6.  Dilead(II) lead(IV) oxide (red lead), $Pb_3O_4$, behaves in many respects as a mixture of lead(II) oxide and lead(IV) oxide and the formula $Pb_2^{II}Pb^{IV}O_4$ (or $2PbO \cdot PbO_2$) is often recommended.  Predict the effect of heat on the substance and write the chemical equation.

7.  Predict the effect of heating separate samples of tin(II) oxide and lead(II) oxide.  Find out what actually happens and write equations.

(Answers on page 63 )

You should also know, in outline, how the other main Group IV oxides are prepared.  Look up the preparations of Group IV oxides in your text-book(s) and then answer the exercise which follows.

Exercise 16  (a)  Which Group IV dioxide(s) cannot be made directly by heating the element in oxygen?

(b)  Which two Group IV monoxides can be prepared by reduction of the dioxide ($XO_2$) by the Group IV element (X)?  Give equations for these reactions.

(c)  Two Group IV monoxides can be prepared by heating the hydroxide or the nitrate.  Give an equation for the formation of each.

(Answers on page **63** )

Now attempt the next exercise which is taken from an A-level question.

Exercise 17  How could:

(a)  carbon monoxide be made from carbon,

(b)  lead monoxide be made from lead?

(Answers on page **63** )

The next exercise deals with selected properties of the oxides of the elements in Group IV.

Exercise 18  (a)  With the aid of your text-book(s) complete a larger copy of Table 11 which you will find on the next page.

(b)  Compare the trends in the stability of the +4 oxides and the +2 oxides as the group is descended.  Do these trends fit with the general patterns for the stability of the +4 and +2 oxidation states that you met earlier?

(c)  What is the relationship between structure and acid-base nature shown by these compounds?

(d)  In general, when elements form oxides in more than one oxidation state, the $MO_2$ oxides are more covalent and slightly more acidic than the corresponding MO oxides.  Is this the case for Group IV oxides?  Illustrate your answer with a pair of oxides.

(e)  Write equations to show the products formed when silicon(IV), tin(IV) and lead(IV) oxides react with alkali.

(f)  Would you expect germanium(IV) oxide to react in the same way?  If so, name the product you would expect and give its formula.

(Answers on page **64** )

Table 11

| Formula | Appearance | Bonding and structure | Acid-base nature | Effect of heat* |
|---|---|---|---|---|
| CO | | | | |
| SiO | This solid is very unstable and not well studied. It disproportionates at room temperature forming $SiO_2$ and Si. Believed to be giant molecular. | | | |
| GeO | Black solid | Mainly ionic, giant ionic | Amphoteric (mainly acidic) | |
| SnO | | | | |
| PbO | | | | |

| Formula | Appearance | Bonding and structure | Acid-base nature | Effect of heat* |
|---|---|---|---|---|
| $CO_2$ | | | | |
| $SiO_2$ | | | | |
| $GeO_2$ | White solid | | | |
| $SnO_2$ | | | | |
| $PbO_2$ | | | | |

*The oxides are heated in air or oxygen.

In the previous exercise you learned that carbon dioxide is a gas consisting of discrete molecules whereas silicon(IV) oxide is a giant molecular solid. The reasons for this sharp contrast in structures are investigated in the next exercise.

Exercise 19   Silicon(IV) oxide (silica) exists in three main polymeric crystalline forms (quartz, tridymite and cristobalite). The crystalline forms are built of tetrahedral units in which the Si atom is surrounded by four oxygen atoms. On the other hand $CO_2$ is a gas consisting of linear molecules.

(a)  Study the following hypothetical conversion and then answer the questions which follow.

Hypothetical polymer        Actual monomer

   (i)   For each carbon dioxide molecule formed, how many C-O bonds are broken in the hypothetical polymer and how many C=O bonds are then made in the carbon dioxide molecule?

   (ii)  The bond energy of C=O in carbon dioxide is approximately 803 kJ $mol^{-1}$ and the bond energy of C-O (general) is 358 kJ/$mol^{-1}$. Use these bond energies to calculate the enthalpy change for the hypothetical reaction.

   (iii) What does the value in (ii) indicate about this change?

(b)  Now consider a similar hypothetical change involving silicon(IV) oxide.

Actual polymer         Hypothetical monomer

The bond energy of Si-O in silicon(IV) oxide is approximately 368 kJ $mol^{-1}$ and the Si=O bond energy is not listed in any data books. Suggest reason(s) for this omission and explain why you think silicon(IV) oxide does not exist as discrete molecules.

(Answers on page 64 )

Silicon is the second most abundant element in the Earth's crust, being widely distributed as silica and silicates. Silica is clearly a very stable substance and this is studied further in the next exercise.

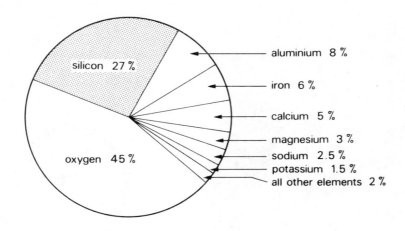

Fig. 10.  Composition of the earth's crust.

Exercise 20  Study Table 12, which lists the enthalpies of formation ($\Delta H_f^{\ominus}$) of the +4 oxides of the elements in Group IV, and answer the questions which follow.

Table 12

| Oxide | $CO_2$ | $SiO_2$ | $GeO_2$ | $SnO_2$ | $PbO_2$ |
|---|---|---|---|---|---|
| $\Delta H_f^{\ominus}$ /kJ mol$^{-1}$ | -394 | -859 (quartz) | -537 | -581 | -277 |

(a)  Which oxide would you expect to be the most stable?

(b)  With reference to the bond energies listed in Table 10 (page 26 ), explain the high stability of the oxide in (a).

(Answers on page **64** )

Compounds containing silicon and oxygen have a wide variety of uses.  Silica in the form of quartz crystals is used to regulate the timing mechanism in electronic clocks and other devices.  Glass made from fused silica resists thermal shock.  Natural silicates and materials made from them are used in the building industry, and silicones are used as lubricants, insulators and protective coatings.

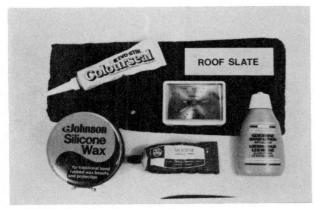

A variety of uses for silicon compounds.

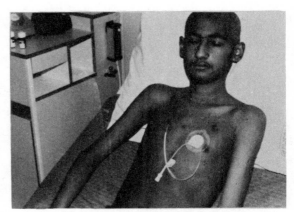

An inert siliconised rubber tube entering the heart. It can remain in the body indefinitely.

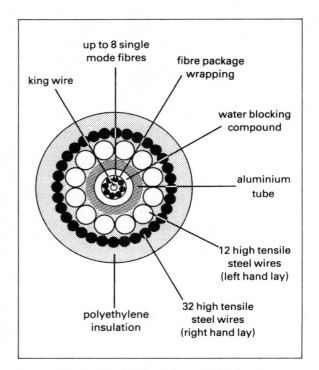

Optical fibres of very pure silica are replacing the more traditional and bulky telephone cables.

Cross-section of torsionally balanced optical cable.

We now move on to consider the halides of Group IV, concentrating mainly on the chlorides.

# Halides of Group IV elements

In this section you examine the structure and bonding of the chlorides, the relative stabilities of the +2 and +4 compounds and the key reactions of the tetrahalides, such as their reaction with water.

You also briefly consider the methods of preparation of the Group IV halides.

Objectives.  When you have finished this section, you should be able to:

(24)  describe briefly the preparations of the dichlorides and tetrachlorides of Group IV;

(25)  describe the preparations of tin(IV) iodide and lead(II) iodide;

(26)  state the structure, bonding, appearance and thermal stabilities of the dichlorides and tetrachlorides;

(27)  explain why tetrachloromethane is resistant to hydrolysis whereas the other Group IV tetrachlorides are hydrolysed.

Read about the methods of preparation of the Group IV chlorides and
of the common iodides of tin and lead (i.e. tin(IV) iodide and
lead(II) iodide).  You have already met the preparation of lead(II)
chloride and lead(II) iodide earlier in this Unit (Experiment 1) and
the preparation of silicon tetrachloride in Unit I3 (The Periodic
Table).  You should also note the appearance, thermal stability, structure
and bonding of these halides.

The next exercise deals with the preparation of the chlorides.  The preparation of the other halides is similar except for lead(IV) bromide and
lead(IV) iodide, which are not known.

Exercise 21  (a)  Complete a larger copy of Table 13.

Table 13

| Formula | Appearance at r.t.p.* | Method of preparation | Equation for preparation |
|---|---|---|---|
| $CCl_4$** | | Pass $Cl_2$ through boiling $CS_2$ | |
| $SiCl_4$** | | | |
| $GeCl_2$ | Colourless solid | | $GeCl_4(g) +$ $Ge(s) \rightleftharpoons$ $2GeCl_2$ $GeCl_2$ dispro-portionates at 75 °C |
| $GeCl_4$ | Fuming colourless liquid | $Cl_2$ over heated Ge | |
| $SnCl_2$ | | | |
| $SnCl_4$ | | | |
| $PbCl_2$ | | | |
| $PbCl_4$ | | | |

*r.t.p. = room temperature and pressure
**The dichlorides of carbon and silicon are not known.

(b)  Which of the dichlorides listed in Table 13 above react
with chlorine at 25 °C to form the tetrachlorides?  Give
a general equation to represent the reactions.

(Answers on page 65.)

Now attempt the next exercise which is taken from an A-level question.

Exercise 22    Tin(IV) iodide (stannic iodide) is prepared by direct
               combination of the elements.

Add 2 g of granulated tin to a solution of 6.35 g of
iodine in 25 cm³ of tetrachloromethane (carbon tetrachloride) in a 100 cm³ flask fitted with a reflux condenser.
Reflux gently until reaction is complete.  Filter through pre-
heated funnel, wash residue with 10 cm³ of hot tetrachloromethane and add washings to the filtrate.  Cool in ice until
orange crystals of tin(IV) iodide separate.  Filter off the
crystals and dry.  The melting-point of tin(IV) iodide is
144 °C.

(Sn = 119, I = 127)

(a)  Write an equation for the reaction.

(b)  Suggest reasons why tetrachloromethane is used.

(c)  Which reactant is in excess?

(d)  Calculate the maximum theoretical yield of product.

(e)  Sketch the apparatus used initially.

(f)  How would you know when reaction is complete?

(g)  Sketch the filtration apparatus, explain why washing is
     necessary and suggest reasons for the procedure adopted.

(h)  How would you obtain a further crop of crystals?

(i)  Sketch the apparatus for determining the melting-point of
     the product and say very briefly how you would measure it.

(j)  Comment on the structure and colour of tin(IV) iodide.

(Answers on page **65** )


In the next exercise you predict the effect of heat in the absence of air
(thermal stability) on the chlorides of Group IV.


Exercise 23    (a)  From your knowledge of the relative stabilities of
                    the +2 and +4 oxidation states of the Group IV
                    compounds and the ease of formation of the
                    chlorides, predict the trend in thermal stability
                    of the tetrachlorides and dichlorides on descending
                    the group.

               (b)  Write equations to show the effect of heat on $SnCl_4$ and
                    $PbCl_4$.

(Answers on page **66** )


We now consider the hydrolysis of the Group IV tetrahalides.


You learned in Unit I3 (The Periodic Table) that tetrachloromethane
is not hydrolysed by water whereas silicon tetrachloride is rapidly
hydrolysed to give hydrated silicon(IV) oxide, $SiO_2 \cdot xH_2O$ (named in
some books as <u>silicic acid</u>).  Read about the hydrolysis of the other
tetrachlorides in the group and find out why tetrachloromethane is
not hydrolysed whereas silicon tetrachloride is hydrolysed.  You should also
note the mechanism for the hydrolysis of silicon tetrachloride.

Now attempt the next exercise, the first part of which is taken from an A-level question.

Exercise 24  (a)  Carbon and silicon are found in the same group of of the Periodic Table.  Their chlorides have the same stoichiometric composition, yet behave differently when treated with water.  Briefly explain this.

(b)  Give the probable mechanism for the hydrolysis of silicon tetrachloride.

(Answers on page **66** )

The next exercise deals with the hydrolysis of the other tetrachlorides in this group.

Exercise 25  The tetrachlorides of germanium, tin and lead are all susceptible to hydrolysis.

(a)  Write a general equation for the hydrolysis of these chlorides.

(b)  Why do you think all the tetrachlorides of Group IV, with the exception of tetrachloromethane, fume in moist air?

(Answers on page **66** )

In Experiment 1 you used $Sn^{2+}(aq)$ and the source of these ions was acidified tin(II) chloride solution.  Find out from your text-book(s) what happens if tin(II) and lead(II) chlorides are dissolved in water and in concentrated hydrochloric acid.

The next exercise deals with the dichlorides of tin and lead.

Exercise 26  (a)  Write an equation to show the reaction between tin(II) chloride and water.

(b)  How does the addition of acid reduce the hydrolysis of tin(II) chloride in water?

(c)  Predict the effect of heat on $SnCl_2 \cdot 2H_2O$.

(d)  Both tin(II) and lead(II) chlorides dissolve in concentrated hydrochloric acid to form complex ions.  Write equations for the formation of these ions.

(Answers on page **67** )

We complete a study of Group IV by asking you to identify, by experiment, some inorganic substances which you have studied in this Unit.

The following 'Observation and deduction exercise', is taken from A-level practical examination papers.  Allow about $1\frac{1}{2}$ hours for this experiment.

## EXPERIMENT 3
Observation and deduction exercise

### Aim

The purpose of this experiment is to give you further practice in the investigation of unknown substances.

### Introduction

The procedure which follows is taken from two separate A-level practical examination papers. Since the format of each paper is slightly different we have divided this experiment into two sections. In the first section you carry out tests on a powder Q, and in the second section you test a solution of a compound H and also a solid I. Note that in the examination, candidates were not told that this experiment referred to Group IV.

### Requirements

safety spectacles
10 test-tubes in rack
test-tube holder
sample of powder Q — — — — — — — — — — — — — — — — — — — — — — — — — — ✖
spatula
Bunsen burner and mat
wood splints and litmus papers
wash-bottle of distilled water
funnel and filter paper
nitric acid, dilute, 2 M $HNO_3$
potassium iodide solution, 0.1 M KI
sodium hydroxide solution, 2 M NaOH
solution of substance H
silver nitrate solution, 0.02 M $AgNO_3$
iron(III) chloride solution (neutralized), 0.3 M $FeCl_3$
potassium thiocyanate solution, 0.5 M KSCN
mercury(II) chloride solution, 0.1 M $HgCl_2$ — — — — — — — — — — — — — — ☠
sample of solid I
1 boiling-tube
sulphuric acid, dilute, 2 M $H_2SO_4$
potassium chromate(VI) solution, 0.5 M $K_2CrO_4$
other chemicals are available from your teacher.

---

### Hazard warning

Mercury(II) chloride solution is poisonous. Therefore you MUST:

AVOID CONTACT WITH SKIN AND DISPOSE OF RESIDUES CONTAINING MERCURY BY POURING INTO THE FUME-CUPBOARD SINK WITH PLENTY OF RUNNING COLD WATER

Procedure

A.  Tests on Q.  Test the powder Q as follows:

1.  Heat a portion in a test-tube until reaction ceases.  Test any gas evolved.

2.  Warm a portion with dilute nitric acid.  Filter if necessary.  Retain the solution or filtrate for (3).

3.  Test portions of the solution or filtrate from (2) with

    (a)  aqueous potassium iodide,

    (b)  aqueous sodium hydroxide.

    Carefully observe what happens, and report fully.  What tentative inferences do you draw from these experiments?  Carry out and report on one further experiment which tests your inferences.  This experiment can be made on Q or on the products of the above reactions.  Full credit will not be given unless your answer discloses the method (including the scale of your experiments), careful observations, and some comment on the type of chemical reactions involved in the experiments.

    The record of your work must be made in (larger copies of) the tables provided.

Results Table 5    Tests with Q

| Test | Method | Observations | Inferences |
|------|--------|-------------|------------|
| (1) Heat | | | |
| (2) Dilute nitric acid | | | |
| (3) Test portions of solution or filtrate from (2) with (a) potassium iodide solution, (b) sodium hydroxide solution. | | | |

Results Table 6    Experiment to test inference

| Inference | Test and Observations | Conclusion |
|-----------|----------------------|------------|
| | | |

(Specimen results on page 66 )

B.  Tests on H and I

    You are provided with a solution of a compound H and a solid I.  Carry out the following tests and record your observations and inferences in a larger copy of Results Table 7.  Then answer the question which follows the table.

Results Table 7

| Test | Observations | Inferences |
|---|---|---|
| 1. To 1 cm³ of the solution of H add aqueous silver nitrate followed by dilute nitric acid. | | |
| 2. To 1 cm³ of the solution of H add aqueous sodium hydroxide until in excess. | | |
| 3. To 1 cm³ of aqueous iron(III) chloride add a few drops of aqueous potassium thiocyanate. To this solution add some of the solution of H. | | |
| 4. To 1 cm³ of aqueous mercury(II) chloride add a little of the solution of H, then excess. | | |
| 5. Heat some of I in a pyrex boiling tube.  Allow to cool. Add 8-10 cm³ of dilute nitric acid to the residue and boil the mixture for 1 or 2 minutes.  Filter if necessary and use portions of the cool solution for the following tests:<br><br>(a) To 1 cm³ of the solution add aqueous sodium hydroxide.<br><br>(b) To 1 cm³ of the solution add dilute sulphuric acid.<br><br>(c) To 1 cm³ of the solution add aqueous potassium chromate(VI) (potassium chromate). | | |

Now answer the following question:

Comment on the nature of the metal contained in H and on the oxidation states of this metal in the compounds involved in reactions 2 to 4.

(Specimen results on page 67 )


You have now completed your study of Group IV.  The following Teacher-marked Exercise will help you to consolidate your knowledge of the group as a whole.

| Teacher-marked Exercise | Survey the chemistry of the Group IV elements (C-Pb) by giving: |  |

A

(a) a summary of the physical and chemical properties of the elements,

(b) brief descriptions of preparative routes of the chlorides and oxides,

(c) a discussion of group trends in valencies and bond-types of the chlorides and oxides,

(d) a discussion of the special properties of carbon and the ways in which its chemistry differs from the other members of the group.

We end this Unit with a brief survey of hydrogen and its position in the Periodic Table.

# HYDROGEN - A UNIQUE ELEMENT

You have already studied many of the compounds of hydrogen in Units I1 (The $s$-block elements), I2 (The Halogens), I3 (The Periodic Table) and in this Unit, the hydrides of Group IV. In addition, you have looked at other special properties of hydrogen such as its emission spectrum in Unit S2 (Atomic Structure) and possibly the behaviour of the hydrogen ion in Unit P3 (Equilibrium II: Acids and Bases). If you have studied Units O2 (Some Functional Groups) and O3 (More Functional Groups) you will have met some of the complex hydrides such as sodium tetrahydroborate(III) (sodium borohydride), $NaBH_4$, and lithium tetrahydridoaluminate(III) (lithium aluminium hydride), $LiAlH_4$, where they are used as reducing agents.

Objective. When you have finished this section, you should be able to:

(28) explain why <u>hydrogen</u> occupies an <u>anomalous and unique</u> position at the top of the Periodic Table.

Hydrogen is made of the simplest atoms and is the most abundant element in the universe, and yet its position in the Periodic Table has been subject to much debate. In many editions of the Periodic Table hydrogen is placed at the top of either Group I or Group VII. It has even been suggested, with imagination, that it could be placed at the head of Group IV.

**Hydrogen is the most abundant element in the universe.**

The next exercise deals with the alleged similarities between hydrogen and the elements in Groups I, IV and VII.

Exercise 27    Complete a larger copy of Table 14 which shows some of the important similarities and differences between hydrogen and the elements in each of the Periodic Groups I, IV and VII. You should base your comparision on the physical and chemical properties of the elements. Group I has been filled in for you in the larger copy to indicate the range of properties you should consider.

(Answers on page 67 )

Table 14

|  | Similarities between hydrogen and a periodic group | Differences between hydrogen and a periodic group |
|---|---|---|
| Group I |  |  |
| Group IV |  |  |
| Group VII |  |  |

It is evident that attempts to classify hydrogen rigidly in these groups is not feasible. Many of the alleged similarities are rather artificial because hydrogen does not closely resemble any other element. It is for this reason that it occupies a unique position at the top of the Periodic Table.

In the next exercise you explore the reasons for the unique nature of hydrogen.

Exercise 28    (a)  Use your data book to write down the following values:

(i)  atomic (covalent) radii of H, Li and F,

(ii)  bond dissociation energies of $H_2$ and $F_2$.

(b)  Why do you think no value is assigned to the ionic radius of the H⁺ ion?

(c)  Why do you think the bond dissociation energies of $H_2$ and $F_2$ are so different?

(d)  What factor(s) do you think are responsible for the unique nature of hydrogen?

(Answers on page 68 )

To consolidate your knowledge about hydrogen attempt the following Teacher-marked Exercise.

Teacher-marked
Exercise

In different forms of the Periodic Table, the element hydrogen is sometimes found to have been placed with the alkali metals, sometimes with the halogens and sometimes alone, at the head of the Periodic Table.

Discuss the relative merits of these three forms of placing hydrogen in the Periodic Table by considering its

(a)  electronic structure,

(b)  physical properties,

(c)  chemical behaviour.

# LEVEL TWO CHECKLIST

You have now reached the end of this Unit.  Look again at the checklist at the end of Level One.  In addition, you should now be able to:

(16)  explain why <u>carbon</u> forms an <u>enormous number of hydrides</u>;

(17)  explain the meaning of the term <u>catenation</u>;

(18)  state the <u>range of hydrides</u> formed by silicon, germanium, tin and lead;

(19)  state the <u>trend</u> in (a) <u>thermal dissociation</u> and (b) <u>reactivity</u> of the <u>tetrahydrides</u> down the group;

(20)  describe the <u>preparation of tin(IV) oxide and lead(IV) oxide</u>;

(21)  describe briefly the preparation of the oxides of the remaining elements in Group IV in the +4 oxidation states;

(22)  state the <u>appearance, acid-base nature, structure and bonding</u> of the <u>oxides</u>;

(23)  give <u>examples</u> to illustrate the <u>relative stabilities</u> of the <u>oxides</u> in the <u>+4 and +2 oxidation states</u>;

(24)  describe briefly the <u>preparations</u> of the <u>tetra- and dichlorides</u> of Group IV;

(25)  describe the <u>preparations of tin(IV) iodide and lead(II) iodide</u>;

(26)  state the <u>structure</u>, <u>bonding</u>, <u>appearance</u> and <u>thermal stabilities</u> of the <u>di- and tetrahalides</u>;

(27)  explain why <u>tetrachloromethane is resistant to hydrolysis</u> whereas the other Group IV <u>tetrachlorides are hydrolysed</u>;

(28)  explain why <u>hydrogen</u> occupies an <u>anomalous and unique position at the top</u> of the Periodic Table.

# END-OF-UNIT TEST

To find out how well you have learned the material in this Unit, try the test which follows.  Read the notes below before starting.

1.  You should spend about $1\frac{1}{2}$ hours on this test.

2.  Hand your answers to your teacher for marking.

# END-OF-UNIT TEST

In Questions 1, 2 and 3 one, or more than one, of the suggested responses may be correct.  Answer as follows.

A  if only 1, 2 and 3 are correct

B  if only 1 and 3 are correct

C  if only 2 and 4 are correct

D  if only 4 is correct

E  if some other response, or combination, is correct.


1.  Which of the following is/are correct statements concerning the trends observed in Group IV of the Periodic Table?

   1  There is an increase in the metallic character of the elements on going down the group.

   2  The stability of the +2 oxidation state increases down the group.

   3  Compounds of lead in the +4 oxidation state are more readily reduced than compounds of carbon in the +4 oxidation state.

   4  The hydrides of lead have greater thermal stability than the hydrides of carbon.                                                    (1)


2.  Arguments in favour of including hydrogen in the halogen group of the Periodic Table are

   1  Hydrogen and chlorine each form a singly charged anion when they combine with the alkali metals.

   2  Molecules of hydrogen are monatomic as are the molecules of all the halogens.

   3  Hydrogen and chlorine can each form covalent compounds with many non-metals.

   4  Hydrogen and chlorine each exist in isotopic forms.                 (1)


3.  Group IV of the Periodic Table comprises the elements carbon, silicon, germanium(Ge), tin and lead.

   It would be expected that

   1  germanium chloride, $GeCl_4$, would be stable towards water

   2  germanium would be formed by the reduction of the oxide $GeO_2$

   3  germanium chloride, $GeCl_4$, would be a strong reducing agent

   4  germanium would react with concentrated nitric acid to give $GeO_2$.  (1)


Questions 4 - 8 concern a laboratory synthesis of tin(IV) iodide. Select the best answer for each question.

$$Sn + 2I_2 \rightarrow SnI_4$$

0.04 mol of tin was refluxed with 0.03 mol of iodine molecules ($I_2$) and 30 cm³ of tetrachloromethane.  Initially the mixture was heated but the reaction was then sufficiently exothermic to continue without further heating.  Towards the end of the preparation, further heat was necessary to ensure that the reaction was complete.  The hot mixture was filtered and orange crystals of tin(IV) iodide were obtained from the filtrate on cooling.

4. One reason for using tetrachloromethane in this preparation would be that

    A  it is a good solvent for tin

    B  it is a good solvent for iodine and tin(IV) iodide

    C  it is not easily hydrolysed

    D  it has a high boiling-point above 250 °C

    E  it is a good catalyst for the reaction between tin and iodine.    (1)

                                               **A**

5. The initial heating of the reaction mixture was necessary because

    A  the reaction is exothermic

    B  air must be removed from the reaction flask

    C  the reactants must be thoroughly mixed

    D  energy must be supplied to overcome the activation energy of the reaction

    E  the tetrachloromethane must be vaporized before any reaction takes place.    (1)

                                                 **A**

6. Assuming the reaction goes to completion, the maximum number of moles of tin(IV) iodide formed would be

    A  0.015    B  0.020    C  0.030    D  0.040    E  0.060

                                               **A**    (1)

7. In order to try to find out if the prepared tin(IV) iodide was pure, it would be best, as a first step, to

    A  investigate its boiling-point

    B  carry out qualitative tests for tin and iodine

    C  carry out a volumetric estimation of the iodide

    D  use a method based on chromatography

    E  investigate its melting-point.    (1)

                                               **A**

8. The best method of finding out when the reaction was complete would be to

    A  measure the boiling-point of the mixture

    B  see when no more tin remained in the reflux flask

    C  note when no more purple fumes of iodine remained in the apparatus

    D  observe when the reaction mixture became colourless

    E  note when no more liquid remained in the reflux flask.    (1)

                                               **A**

Questions 9 and 10 are followed by five suggested answers. Select the best answer in each case.

9. Hydrogen has sometimes been included in Group I of the Periodic Table and sometimes in Group VII.

   Which statement could NOT be used to justify its inclusion in one or other of these groups?

   A  Hydrogen can form a hydrated cation.

   B  Hydrogen can form an anion.

   C  Hydrogen is a diatomic gas.

   D  Hydrogen is a good reducing agent.

   E  Hydrogen has a zero electrode potential.                                   (1)

10. Which of the following statements is true for hydrogen but for no other element?

    A  Hydrogen is never reduced.

    B  In reacting with other elements, hydrogen forms both positive and simple negative ions.

    C  In reacting with other elements, hydrogen forms both covalent and electrovalent bonds.

    D  In reacting with other elements, hydrogen forms an ion containing two electrons only.

    E  Hydrogen forms electrovalent bonds with alkali metals.                    (1)

11. Group IV of the Periodic Table contains the elements carbon, silicon, germanium, tin and lead in increasing order of atomic number. The most common oxidation states for this group are -4, +2 and +4.

    (a) Write the formula of a hydride of silicon in the -4 oxidation state.                                                                       (1)

    (b) Write an equation representing the thermal decomposition of the compound in (a).                                                            (2)

    (c) Put the hydrides of this group in order of increasing stability to heat (i.e. put the MOST stable LAST).                                    (2)

    (d) Silicon hydride burns SPONTANEOUSLY in air forming silica.

        (i)  Write the equation for this reaction.                              (2)

        (ii) If the conditions of reaction (i) are compared with the combustion of methane, in what way does this confirm your answer in (c)?                                                        (2)

    (e) Place the oxides of the element in this group (all in the +4 oxidation state) in order of increasing acidity (i.e. put the MOST acidic LAST). Give an explanation of the order listed.                          (3)

12.  This question concerns the elements of Group IV of the Periodic Table:  carbon, silicon, germanium, tin and lead.

(a)  (i)  The tetrachlorides of these elements have the same molecular shape.  What is this shape, and what is the nature of the bonding present in the molecules?

(ii)  Silicon tetrachloride reacts vigorously with water.  Give an equation for this reaction.

Unlike silicon tetrachloride, carbon tetrachloride does not react with water.  Explain this difference in behaviour.  (5)

(b)  Give the structures of carbon dioxide and silicon dioxide.  (3)

(c)  (i)  Tin(II) compounds show reducing properties.  Give ONE example of this behaviour, and write an equation for the reaction.

(ii)  Lead(IV) oxide has oxidizing properties.  Describe ONE example of this behaviour, and write an equation for the reaction.  (4)

(d)  When dilute hydrochloric acid is added to a solution of lead(II) nitrate, a white precipitate is formed, but, if concentrated acid is used, much less precipitate is formed.

(i)  What is the white solid formed?  Write an ionic equation.

(ii)  Explain the difference in behaviour.  (4)

13.  The elements in Group IV of the Periodic Table are C, Si, Ge, Sn and Pb.

(a)  Write down the formulae of the simple chlorides of these elements.  In each case state whether the chloride is solid, liquid or gaseous at room temperature and pressure.  Note that some of the elements form more than one simple chloride.  (4)

(b)  Select from your list in (a), (i) a chloride which is essentially covalent, and (ii) a chloride which is essentially ionic.  For each of these  describe briefly but clearly how you would prepare it from readily available materials.  (5)

14.  The atomic numbers of carbon, silicon, germanium, tin and lead are 6, 14, 32, 50 and 82 respectively.

(a)  (i)  Give the electron configuration of silicon and predict that of tin.

(ii)  Which of the five elements has the greatest total ionization energy for the process $M(g) \rightarrow M^{2+}(g)$?  Explain your reasoning.  (4)

(b)  All five elements exhibit a covalency of four but compounds containing the ions $M^{4+}$ or $M^{4-}$ are rare.

(i)  How do you account for this?

(ii)  Which of these elements is most likely to form $M^{4-}$ ions?  Give your reasons.  (4)

(c)  Germanium, tin and lead can also exhibit an oxidation state of +2.  How do you account for this?  (2)

(d)  Carbon atoms are able to form chains to a greater extent than the other elements.  Suggest an explanation for this.  (3)

(Total 60 marks)

# APPENDIX

<u>Lead Pollution</u>

This topic may not be on your syllabus but we hope you will work through it since it is an issue which demonstrates the impact of chemistry on society.

You probably know (from newspapers, science magazines, television and radio) that lead pollution has reached levels which many scientists and doctors believe will have, or are having, widespread adverse effects on public health.  There is much debate about the acceptable limits of lead in our environment and you might find it useful to discuss the problem of lead pollution with other people who are interested in this topic.

The passage on pages 54 and 55 is an extract from a book entitled 'The Biochemistry of Pollution'.  You will find it a useful starting point for your discussions.  In any case you should read it carefully and answer the following exercises.

The first exercise deals with some of the uses of lead which are responsible for pollution.

### 3.4.2 Lead pollution

The toxicity of lead has been known for a long time. Formerly, the chief sources of lead poisoning were lead-based paints, often ingested by children, and lead storage tanks and pipes carrying drinking water.

Lead plumbing has been used at least since Roman times. It has been seriously suggested (though not often accepted) that the decline of the Roman Empire was due to the infertility of Roman matrons exposed to lead poisoning from their plumbing. The extent to which Pb dissolves depends on the hardness of the water; several ppm can be found in water that is soft and slightly acid, especially if it contains natural chelating agents (humic acids) derived from peat. Recent studies from the Glasgow area have suggested that children of mothers living in soft-water areas are more likely to suffer from mental retardation. Although lead is very poorly absorbed from the gut, it is a cumulative poison, and can accumulate in bone (with exchange into plasma) over many years.

The situation has changed completely since the intensive use of the petrol engine, beginning about 1910, when the start of a rise in the Pb content of circumpolar snow can be demonstrated. The four-stroke petrol engine makes very strict demands on its fuel – it must vaporize readily when drawn into the cylinder, but burn relatively slowly when ignited. Explosion ('knocking') leads to lowered efficiency, overheating of the cylinder, and mechanical stress (see BAILEY et al., 1979)

Straight-chain hydrocarbons of the correct volatility, such as $n$-heptane ($C_7H_{16}$), are very poor fuels, largely because the initial reaction with $O_2$ produces 'free radicals' (molecular fragments containing an unbonded electron). If more than one free radical is produced at each step, the combustion rate increases autocatalytically. Branched-chain hydrocarbons such as iso-octane burn much more slowly, because multiple free radical formation stops at the branch points. Unfortunately, even the most sophisticated refining technology does not produce enough branched-chain hydrocarbons of the right volatility for petrol engines. (Diesel engines do not suffer from this problem.)

The solution has been to slow down the rate of combustion by using substances known as chain-breakers or scavengers ('anti-knock agents'), the most successful of which are tetraethyl- and tetramethyl-lead. As much as 0.8 ml of such compounds have been added to each litre of petrol, equivalent to about 2 g Pb litre$^{-1}$; the present European limit is about 0.5 g litre$^{-1}$. The total amounts of lead used are staggering – 300 000 tonnes a year in the U.S.A., 50 000 tonnes a year in the U.K.

Lead tetra-alkyls are themselves extremely poisonous, volatile compounds, affecting the central nervous system, but it is the inorganic lead in the products of combustion which gives cause for concern. Fine particles of lead metal or lead halides are emitted and taken up into the lungs. Lead appears to be absorbed very much more efficiently into the bloodstream from the lungs than from the intestine.

Most of the lead particles fall to earth within a relatively short distance of the roadway. Both airborne particles and the lead-contaminated foliage are much reduced after a distance of about 150 m from the road. Airborne lead pollution is therefore essentially an urban (or motorway) problem. It has been very difficult to decide how serious it is because of the imprecision of the clinical symptoms to be expected in people suffering from sub-acute lead poisoning.

The symptoms of severe lead poisoning are well known. The most characteristic are a painful intestinal colic (spasm), loss of function in peripheral nerves leading to tremors and paralysis, failure of kidney function, and convulsions, which may be fatal. If poisoning is chronic, there may be anaemia. All but the most severe cases can be cured by prolonged treatment with a chelating agent such as EDTA. It is, however, worrying that some children who have contracted acute lead poisoning, and have been treated until their clinical symptoms have disappeared, have much later shown evidence of emotional difficulties and mental retardation. Evidence connecting the latter with high levels of lead in drinking water has already been mentioned, and the blood lead levels in children kept in institutions because of emotional instability are often high. All this suggests that exposure to lead may have a long-term effect, to which children are particularly susceptible, persisting after clinical symptoms have been relieved.

Unfortunately the milder forms of the symptoms described above – fatigue, depression, digestive upsets and mental retardation – are hard to quantify, as many of us often suffer from the first three. How does one tell whether a city-dweller is suffering from sub-acute lead poisoning which may have a lasting, if delayed, effect? Two approaches have been used. One is to measure the lead concentration in the blood of city-dwellers, and to compare the results with those found in clinically-defined lead poisoning. Figure 3–3 shows that, at least in the late 1960s, the lead concentration in the blood of city children was disturbingly high, although probably never equal to the threshold value for the appearance of clinical symptoms. The lower values indicated on the graph, the 'toxic thresholds', are disputed

tion of the central nervous system. Anaemia, as a result of lead poisoning, occurs rather late, whereas the nervous symptoms appear early, and are almost certainly not due to anoxia.

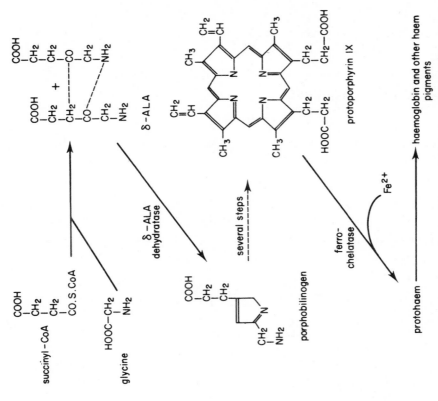

**Fig. 3–4** Stages in the synthesis of haem. δ-ALA is an abbreviation for δ-aminolaevulinic acid, which can be detected in urine if the enzyme δ-ALA dehydratase is inhibited by lead.

because they correspond to the mild symptoms which are so hard to evaluate. It is also noteworthy that the blood lead concentration in the *average* inhabitant of Los Angeles is the same as that of natives of New Guinea. The concentration of Pb in the milk teeth of children is more accurately diagnostic; it is distinctly high in urban children.

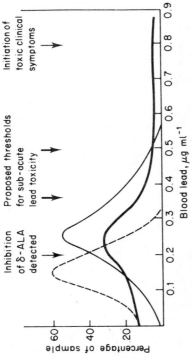

**Fig. 3–3** Distribution of blood lead content from urban populations. – – – – represents adult males living in the suburbs, ——— represents adult males living in the city centre, (both samples taken in Philadelphia, 1961–2), ——— represents normal children living in the Manchester area (1966–7). The results for the latter are not normally distributed, and the graph shows signs that it could be decomposed into two curves, for inner-city and suburban inhabitants, corresponding to those for the USA males. The outer arrows represent respectively the concentrations at which inhibition of δ-aminolaevulinic acid can be detected (left), and the threshold for the initiation of toxic clinical symptoms (right). The central arrows indicate blood lead concentrations which have been proposed as thresholds for sub-acute lead toxicity.

The other approach is to see if there is any biochemical lesion that can be used as an indicator. $Pb^{2+}$ inhibits many enzymes, but especially those connected with the synthesis of haem, shown diagrammatically in Fig. 3–4. It is well-established that lead poisoning leads to a raised excretion of δ-aminolaevulinic acid (ALA) and porphobilinogen, and that free porphyrin accumulates in red blood cells. The excretion of ALA is the most sensitive indicator of lead poisoning, but it does not correlate at all well with the symptoms that cause most concern – those due to malfunc-

Exercise 29  (a)  List three uses of lead which can result in the pollution of the environment.

(b)  Which of the three uses listed in (a) is chiefly responsible for lead pollution today?

(c)  Name the lead-containing compounds which are added to petrol.

(d)  Why are these lead compounds added to petrol?

(Answers on page **68**)


The next exercise is concerned with the health hazards associated with lead pollution.


Exercise 30  (a)  State two ways in which lead can be absorbed into the bloodstream.  Which is more efficient?

(b)  It has been suggested that lead pollution is a greater health risk for people living near busy roads.

(i)  What evidence (if any) supports this view?

(ii)  Are the risks spread evenly over the whole age-range of the population?

(c)  What are the symptoms of severe lead poisoning?

(d)  What do you think the author of the article means by sub-acute lead poisoning?

(e)  Why do you think the acceptable limits of lead in our environment are continuously under debate?

(Answers on page **68**)


The next exercise is concerned with the methods employed for detecting lead in the human body.


Exercise 31  (a)  State briefly the methods which have been used in an attempt to diagnose mild lead poisoning.

(b)  Which method can be used for determining lead concentration only in children?

(Answers on page **68**)


To consolidate your knowledge on lead pollution, attempt the following Teacher-marked Exercise which is taken from an A-level paper.  Read the question carefully and then discuss with your teacher, and other interested people, any points which you might not have covered.

56

Teacher-marked
Exercise

Read the following statements and answer the questions below.

A   If the human body gains more lead than it loses, lead intoxication sets in.

B   European Economic Community (EEC) legislation has limited the lead content of petrol to 0.4 g $l^{-1}$ (g $dm^{-3}$).

C   Some mentally retarded children were found to have more lead in their bodies than those of normal children.

D   The Romans may have suffered chronic lead poisoning due to the use of lead pots for boiling grape juice in preparing sweetened wine.

E   Some experts suggest that about five times as much lead is absorbed from the food we eat as from the air we breathe.

F   The air in an industrial area may be polluted by lead from various sources.

(a)    (i)   Name two processes by which lead is removed from the body.

       (ii)  Name two fluids which might be examined to check the extent of lead intoxication in the body.

       (iii) In what units might the extent of lead intoxication be reported?

(b)   State one advantage and one disadvantage of the EEC legislation.

(c)   On the basis of C, it is possible to suggest that lead poisoning is the cause of mental retardation.

       (i)   Would you support this suggestion?  Briefly explain your answer.

       (ii)  Give one other explanation of the statement made in C above.

(d)    (i)   Explain briefly how you might determine experimentally the average lead intake from wine consumed by the Romans.  (Note that lead(II) sulphate is very sparingly soluble in water.)

       (ii)  Give two facts that you would need to know to arrive at an estimate of the lead intake of, say, Julius Caesar.

(e)   State three specific sources of lead in the food we eat.

(f)   State two different sources of lead in polluted air.

# ANSWERS

(Answers to questions from examination papers are provided by ILPAC and not by the Examination Boards.)

## Exercise 1

(a) Electronic configuration of

  (i)   Sn is    $1s^2 2s^2 2p^6 3s^2 3p^6 3d^{10} 4s^2 4p^6 4d^{10} 5s^2 5p^2$

         Sn²⁺ is   $1s^2 2s^2 2p^6 3s^2 3p^6 3d^{10} 4s^2 4p^6 4d^{10} 5s^2$

  (ii)  Pb is   $1s^2 2s^2 2p^6 3s^2 3p^6 3d^{10} 4s^2 4p^6 4d^{10} 4f^{14} 5s^2 5p^6 5d^{10} 6s^2 6p^2$

         Pb²⁺ is   $1s^2 2s^2 2p^6 3s^2 3p^6 3d^{10} 4s^2 4p^6 4d^{10} 4f^{14} 5s^2 5p^6 5d^{10} 6s^2$

(b) The outer s electrons are unaffected in the formation of Sn²⁺ and Pb²⁺ ions.

(c) Carbon and silicon do not contain d-electrons.

(d) Eight electrons could occupy the outer shell of carbon, 18 electrons could occupy the outer shell of silicon.

This is because there are no d-orbitals in the second shell (thus C is limited to 8 electrons), whereas d-orbitals are available in the third shell (thus Si can have a maximum of 18 electrons).

## Exercise 2

(a) Table 3

| Element | Ionization energies/kJ mol⁻¹ | | | | |
|---|---|---|---|---|---|
| | 1st | 2nd | 3rd | 4th | 5th |
| C | 1090 | 2350 | 4610 | 6220 | 37800 |
| Si | 786 | 1580 | 3230 | 4360 | 16000 |
| Ge | 762 | 1540 | 3300 | 4390 | 8950 |
| Sn | 707 | 1410 | 2940 | 3930 | 7780 |
| Pb | 716 | 1450 | 3080 | 4080 | 6700 |

(Note that values may differ from source to source.)

(b) The first ionization energy drops sharply, then gradually, and then becomes nearly constant. This is in line with the dramatic increase in atomic radius from carbon to silicon followed by a gradual increase in atomic radius from silicon to lead. It is particularly difficult to remove an outer electron from the small carbon atom since it is only shielded from the nucleus by two inner electrons. The outer electrons in silicon are shielded from the nucleus by two full shells of electrons (i.e. 2 and 8) and are further from the nucleus.

From silicon downwards the effective nuclear pull on the outer electrons gradually decreases since atomic size increases gradually and the screening effect improves.

(Continued above right.)

---

(c) Yes, the successive ionization energies increase since the removal of an electron at each stage increases the effective nuclear pull on the remaining outer electrons. The jump between the 4th and 5th ionization energies occurs after all four outer electrons have been removed and the fifth electron is removed from an inner shell, so that a great deal more energy is required.

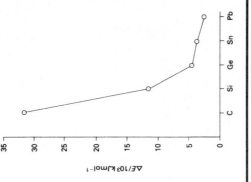

(d) The sharp drop from carbon to silicon occurs because in carbon the fifth electron is removed from the first shell which contains two electrons. Clearly, removal of one of these electrons is extremely difficult due to their closeness to the nucleus, whereas in silicon the 5th electron is removed from the 2nd shell which is further from the nucleus and is shielded by two electrons. The drop from silicon to germanium is also large because the 5th electron to be removed from germanium is fairly well shielded by the inner electrons and further away. The gradual drop from Ge → Sn → Pb is in line with the gradual increase in atomic size and the improved shielding effect.

## Exercise 3

(a) Carbon - it is far more difficult to remove electrons from this atom compared to the other atoms because of its small size.

(b) Carbon. (Note: the converse must not be assumed. The ions Pb⁴⁺ and Sn⁴⁺ probably do not exist in any significant quantity. Pb(IV) and Sn(IV) compounds have a high percentage of covalent character.)

(c) Carbon - it is least likely to lose electrons.

(d) Tin and lead are likely to show metallic character since they are most likely to lose electrons. (Note that the ionization energies suggest surprisingly that silicon may be more metallic than lead - but ionization energy is not the sole factor. If enthalpies of atomization are added to the first two ionization energies for each element, the totals are more or less equal, showing equal ease of ion formation from the crystalline element.)

(e) No - all have similar 1st and 2nd ionization energies, and there is no dramatic increase between the 2nd and 3rd ionization energies for tin and lead.

## Exercise 4

(a) The co-ordination number in the diamond structure is 4 and for the graphite structure it is 3.

(b) The diamond structure contains puckered six-membered rings of carbon atoms, which are linked together in sheets or planes, like the flat six-membered rings of graphite.

(a) Melting-points drop sharply and then gradually decrease, with the exception of Pb. The boiling-points also drop sharply and then gradually decrease (bearing in mind the uncertain data for the boiling-points for all the Group IV elements except Pb).

(b) The trend in (a) suggests that the cohesive forces between the atoms decrease as the Group is descended.

(c) (i) The large decrease in melting-point and boiling-point from carbon (diamond) to silicon is closely linked to the dramatic difference between $E$(Si-Si) and $E$(C-C). (The structures of both diamond and silicon are similar.)

   (ii) The drop in the element-element bond energies from silicon to germanium to tin (white) is more gradual and this is reflected in the gradual decrease in the melting-points.

(d) The enthalpies of atomization would be expected to drop sharply and then gradually decrease as the Group is descended, as do the melting-points and boiling-points.

(e) Lead has a lower bond energy than tin and therefore has a lower enthalpy of atomization. The process of melting does not separate atoms whereas atomization does; thus although both processes are dependent on bond energies, differences in structure have a more marked effect on melting-points than on enthalpies of atomization. Since lead has a typical metallic close-packed structure whereas tin (white) has a more open and irregular structure, this difference in structure is more likely to raise the melting-point of lead than enthalpy of atomization.

Exercise 7

(a) Table 6

| Element | | Electrical conductivity | Hardness and malleability |
|---|---|---|---|
| C | Graphite | Fairly good | Soft and slippery |
| | Diamond | Non conductor | Very hard and brittle |
| Si | | Semi-conductor | Hard and brittle |
| Ge | | Semi-conductor | Hard and brittle |
| Sn | Grey (α) | Semi-conductor | Hard and brittle |
| | White (β) | Good conductor | Soft and malleable |
| Pb | | Good conductor | Soft and malleable |

(b) Carbon.

(c) Lead.

(Electronegativity is a very qualitative concept and it seems to accept a slight progressive decrease from Si to Pb. However, there is some arguable evidence to suggest that germanium is more electronegative than silicon and lead.)

Exercise 5

(a) Table 4

| | | Density/g cm$^{-3}$ | Structure | Bonding |
|---|---|---|---|---|
| C | Diamond | 3.51 | Giant atomic diamond structure | Covalent |
| | Graphite | 2.25 | Layer structure | Covalent |
| Si | | 2.33 (value uncertain) | Giant atomic diamond structure | Covalent |
| Ge | | 5.35 | Giant atomic diamond structure | Covalent |
| Sn | Grey (α) | 5.75 | Giant atomic diamond structure | Covalent |
| | White (β) | 7.28 | Tetragonal (distorted close-packed) | Metallic |
| Pb | | 11.3 | F.C.C. (close-packed) | Metallic |

(b) With the exception of silicon (whose value is uncertain) and graphite, density increases with increasing atomic number.

(c) Diamond, silicon, germanium and grey tin all have a covalent diamond structure whereas white tin and lead have a metallic structure. Graphite at the top of the group is also covalent but it has a layer structure.

(d) In general, the increase in density from diamond down to grey tin is related to the increasing mass of the individual atoms (all these elements have the same structure). The density of graphite is less than that of diamond since graphite has a more open structure. The metallic structures of tin and lead are more close-packed than the diamond structure, therefore white tin and lead are denser than grey tin and the preceding elements. White tin is less dense than lead because its atoms have a smaller mass and its structure is distorted (and therefore more open).

(e) The transition temperature, i.e. the temperature at which grey tin and white tin are in equilibrium, is 13.2 °C. However, transformation is observable only after long exposure to lower temperatures.

Table 9

| Reagent | General Reaction | Comments | | | | |
|---|---|---|---|---|---|---|
| | | Carbon | Silicon | Germanium | Tin | Lead |
| Oxygen | $X + O_2 \rightarrow XO_2$ Except Pb ($\rightarrow$ PbO). | Burns at red heat. | Burns at red heat. | Slow at red heat. | Slow at white heat. | PbO formed at 400 °C. |
| Chlorine | $X + 2Cl_2 \rightarrow XCl_4$ Except Pb ($\rightarrow$ PbCl$_2$). | No reaction. | SiCl$_4$ on heating. | GeCl$_4$ on heating. | SnCl$_4$ on heating. | PbCl$_2$ on heating. |
| Water | $X + 2H_2O \rightarrow XO_2 + 2H_2$ Except C ($\rightarrow$ CO) and Pb ($\rightarrow$ moderately soluble Pb(OH)$_2$ in aerated soft water, $\overline{PbSO_4(s)}$ in hard). | Hot C and steam form CO + H$_2$. | Hot Si + steam react. | Very hot Ge and steam react slightly, if at all. | White hot Sn and steam react. | Hardly any reaction with steam in the absence of air. |
| Alkalis | H$_2$ and oxo-anion* salts formed. | No reaction. | Hot conc. alkali needed. | Hot conc. alkali needed. | Slow in hot conc. alkali. | Molten alkali needed. |
| Conc. hydro-chloric acid | $X + 2H^+ \rightarrow X^{2+} + H_2$ | No reaction. | No reaction. | No reaction. | Moderate reaction in hot acid. | Moderate reaction in boiling acid. |

*Silicate(IV), germanate(IV), mainly stannate(II) and plumbate(II) salts formed as appropriate.

Exercise 8

(a) Table 7

| Element | | Uses of element | Physical property employed |
|---|---|---|---|
| C | Diamond | Gemstones | Light reflecting and refracting properties |
| | | Cutting tools | Hardness |
| | | Abrasives | Hardness |
| | Graphite | Lubricants | Softness and 'slip' |
| | | Pencils | Opacity and 'slip' |
| | | Electrodes | Electrical conductivity and chemical inertness |
| Si | | Transistors Computers Rectifiers | Semi-conductivity |
| Sn(white) | | Tin-plating steel | Resistance to corrosion and non-toxicity |
| | | Solders (alloys of Sn, Pb and Sb) | Low melting-point and resistance to corrosion |
| Pb | | Car batteries | Electrical conductivity (and chemical properties) |
| | | Radiation shields | High density |
| | | Roofing | Malleability and resistance to corrosion |
| | | Solders | Resistance to corrosion and low melting-point |

Exercise 9

(a) Table 9 (see opposite).

(b) (i) The common oxidation state of lead in its compounds is +2.

(ii) The common oxidation states of tin are +4 and +2.

(c) Yes. Tin and lead show metallic character in that they react with hydrochloric acid to produce hydrogen. Furthermore lead forms divalent lead ions in aerated soft water.

(d) Lead dissolves in soft water to form lead ions. Soluble lead compounds are harmful.

Experiment 1. Specimen results

Results Table 1

| Acid | Tin | Lead |
|---|---|---|
| Dilute hydrochloric acid | Colourless gas evolved on heating which 'popped' with a lighted splint. | Slight reaction (if any) on heating. |
| Concentrated hydrochloric acid | Colourless gas evolved on heating which 'popped' with a lighted splint. | Colourless gas evolved on heating. 'Popped' with difficulty. White solid produced in test-tube. |
| Concentrated nitric acid | Brown gas evolved on heating. | Brown gas evolved on heating. |

Results Table 2

| Reagent | $Sn^{2+}(aq)$ (acidified) | $Pb^{2+}(aq)$ |
|---|---|---|
| (a) Sodium hydroxide solution | White precipitate dissolved in excess sodium hydroxide solution. | White precipitate dissolved in excess sodium hydroxide solution. |
| (b) Ammonia solution | White precipitate insoluble in excess ammonia solution. | White precipitate insoluble in excess ammonia solution. |
| (c) Dilute hydrochloric acid | No reaction. | White precipitate dissolved on boiling and crystallized on cooling to form white crystals. |
| (d) Acidified potassium manganate(VII) solution | Decolorized | No reaction. |
| (e) Potassium chromate solution | Green-blue solution obtained. | Yellow precipitate formed. |
| (f) Sodium sulphide solution | Brown precipitate formed. | Dark brown-black precipitate formed. |
| (g) Potassium iodide solution | No reaction. | Yellow precipitate formed. |

Experiment 1. Questions

1. (a) $Pb(s) + 2HCl(aq) \rightarrow PbCl_2(s) + H_2(g)$    ($PbCl_2(aq)$ if hot)

   $Sn(s) + 2HCl(aq) \rightarrow SnCl_2(aq) + H_2(g)$

2. Yes, metals above hydrogen in the electrochemical series produce hydrogen on reaction with acids.

3. (a) Nitrogen dioxide($NO_2$) is responsible for the brown colour.

   (b) Yes, zinc (or copper) reacts in a similar way.

   (c) Nitric acid is a strong oxidizing agent.

4. Table 8

| Equations | Comments |
|---|---|
| $Sn^{2+}(aq) + 2OH^-(aq) \rightarrow Sn(OH)_2(s)$<br>$Sn(OH)_2(s) + 4OH^-(aq) \rightarrow Sn(OH)_6^{4-}(aq)$ | The precipitate dissolves in excess NaOH to form a stannate(II) ion* $Sn(OH)_6^{4-}$. |
| $Pb^{2+}(aq) + 2OH^-(aq) \rightarrow Pb(OH)_2(s)$<br>$Pb(OH)_2(s) + 4OH^-(aq) \rightarrow Pb(OH)_6^{4-}(aq)$ | The precipitate dissolves in excess NaOH to form a plumbate(II) ion $Pb(OH)_6^{4-}$. |
| $2MnO_4^-(aq) + 16H^+(aq) + 5Sn^{2+}(aq) \rightarrow 2Mn^{2+}(aq) + 5Sn^{4+}(aq)*** + 8H_2O(l)$ | Redox reaction. $Sn^{2+}$ is behaving as a reducing agent. |
| $Pb^{2+}(aq) + 2Cl^-(aq) \rightarrow PbCl_2(s)$ | Simple precipitation reaction. Precipitate soluble in hot water. |
| $Cr_2O_7^{2-}(aq)** + 14H^+(aq) + 3Sn^{2+}(aq) \rightarrow 2Cr^{3+}(aq) + 3Sn^{4+}(aq)*** + 7H_2O(l)$ | Redox reaction. $Sn^{2+}$ is behaving as a reducing agent. $Cr^{3+}$ gives the solution its blue-green colour. |
| $Pb^{2+}(aq) + CrO_4^{2-}(aq) \rightarrow PbCrO_4(s)$ | Simple precipitation reaction. |
| $Pb^{2+}(aq) + S^{2-}(aq) \rightarrow PbS(s)$ | Simple precipitation reaction. |
| $Sn^{2+}(aq) + S^{2-}(aq) \rightarrow SnS(s)$ | Simple precipitation reaction. |
| $Pb^{2+}(aq) + 2I^-(aq) \rightarrow PbI_2(s)$ | Simple precipitation reaction. The precipitate is soluble in hot water and recrystallizes on cooling as golden yellow platelets. |

*Various formulae have been proposed for the stannate(II) ion ranging from $SnO_2^{2-}$ for the anhydrous form to $Sn(OH)_4^{2-}$ and $Sn(OH)_6^{4-}$ for the hydrated forms. $Sn(OH)_6^{4-}$ seems the most probable. Similar variations have been proposed for the plumbate(II) ion, $Pb(OH)_6^{4-}$.

**Chromate(VI) ($CrO_4^{2-}$) changes to dichromate(VI) ($Cr_2O_7^{2-}$) when acidified ($2CrO_4^{2-}(aq) + 2H^+(aq) \rightleftharpoons Cr_2O_7^{2-}(aq) + H_2O(l)$).

***$Sn^{4+}$ ions are stated in the equations for convenience; you should bear in mind that tin(IV) compounds are mainly covalent. Aqueous solutions of tin(IV) usually contain complexes.

Experiment 1. Questions (continued)

5. If potassium manganate(VII) solution were acidified with hydrochloric acid or sulphuric acid the chloride or sulphate ions would react with the lead ions to form a white precipitate of lead(II) chloride or lead(II) sulphate.

$$Pb^{2+}(aq) + 2Cl^-(aq) \rightarrow PbCl_2(s)$$
$$Pb^{2+}(aq) + SO_4^{2-}(aq) \rightarrow PbSO_4(s)$$

Ethanoate ions will not form a precipitate with lead ions.

6. Lead(II) ions are more stable because they are not oxidized by any of the reagents used in the experiment. Tin(II) ions are oxidized to the +4 state by acidified solutions of potassium manganate(VII) and potassium dichromate(VI).

7. The tin(II) ions are likely to be oxidized by the mercury(II) chloride forming the tin(IV) compound and mercury. The final appearance of the mixture is therefore likely to be grey due to the formation of mercury. This does in fact occur, although mercury(I) chloride ($Hg_2Cl_2$) is initially formed as a white solid.

$$2HgCl_2(aq) + Sn^{2+}(aq) \rightarrow Hg_2Cl_2(s) + Sn^{4+}(aq) + 2Cl^-(aq)$$
$$Hg_2Cl_2(s) + Sn^{2+}(aq) \rightarrow 2Hg(l) + Sn^{4+}(aq) + 2Cl^-(aq)$$

Exercise 10

(a) The more stable oxidation state of tin is +4.

(b) (i) No. The +2 state is far less stable than the +4 state.

(ii) Yes. Although the +4 state is less stable than the +2 state the difference in stability is not so great as in the cases of carbon and silicon.

(c) The inert pair effect.

Exercise 11

(a) Silicon forms a range of hydrides from $SiH_4$ to $Si_6H_{14}$. Germanium forms a range of hydrides from $GeH_4$ to $Ge_9H_{20}$. Tin forms two hydrides: $SnH_4$ and $Sn_2H_6$. Lead forms one hydride: $PbH_4$.

(b) Catenation is the formation of chains consisting of element-element bonds. Carbon is the element showing the greatest tendency to catenation.

(c) Yes, the bonding in the other Group IV hydrides is similar to the alkanes.

(d) All the Group IV tetrahydrides are composed of tetrahedral molecules.

Exercise 12

(a) Carbon, (b) Carbon, (c) Carbon, (d) Carbon.

(e) The hydrides of carbon are least readily oxidized. The changes in enthalpy (and free energy) associated with combustion of these hydrides might be expected to have the smallest negative values because combustion requires the breaking of X-H bonds (strongest for C) and the formation of X-O bonds (weakest for C).

Exercise 12 (continued)

(e) (The fact that C=O bonds are formed does not alter the argument substantially since $E(C=O) = 800$ kJ mol$^{-1}$. This point is pursued in Exercise 20.)

Exercise 13

(a) The alkenes contain a C=C bond.
The alkynes contain a C≡C bond.

(b) No. Group IV elements, apart from carbon, do not form hydrides corresponding to the alkenes and alkynes.

Exercise 14

(a) Thermal stability drops sharply from $CH_4$ to $SiH_4$ and then gradually decreases.

(b) Yes, this is in line with the decreasing stability of the tetravalent state as the group is descended.

Exercise 15

(a) Reactivity of the tetrahydrides increases as the group is descended.

(b) $SiH_4(g) + 2O_2(g) \rightarrow SiO_2(s) + 2H_2O(g)$.

Experiment 2. Specimen results

Results Table 3

| | |
|---|---|
| Mass of Pb | 5.0 g |
| Mass of $PbO_2$ | 3.9 g |
| % yield | 67% |
| Appearance of $PbO_2$ | Red/brown solid |
| Appearance of $SnO_2$ | White/pale yellow solid |

Percentage yield of $PbO_2$ is calculated as follows:

1 mol of Pb produces 1 mol of $PbO_2$

i.e. 207 g of Pb produces 239 g of $PbO_2$

∴ 1 g of Pb produces $\frac{239 \text{ g}}{207}$ of $PbO_2$

∴ 5.0 g of Pb produces $\frac{239 \text{ g}}{207} \times 5.0 = 5.8$ g of $PbO_2$ (theoretical maximum)

$$\% \text{ yield} = \frac{\text{actual mass of product}}{\text{theoretical mass of product}} \times 100$$

∴ $\% \text{ yield} = \frac{3.9 \text{ g}}{5.8 \text{ g}} \times 100 = \boxed{67\%}$

## Experiment 2. Questions (continued)

7. Tin(II) oxide might be expected to combine with oxygen on heating, to form tin(IV) oxide because the +4 oxidation state is generally more stable for tin. This happens in practice:

$$2SnO(s) + O_2(g) \rightarrow 2SnO_2(s)$$

A similar oxidation of lead(II) oxide to lead(IV) oxide would not be expected because the latter decomposes on heating (see Question 1) and the +2 oxidation is generally more stable for lead.

In practice, prolonged heating in air at about 400 °C causes partial oxidation to dilead(II) lead(IV) oxide, $Pb_3O_4$, which decomposes again at higher temperatures.

$$6PbO(s) + O_2(g) \rightleftharpoons 2Pb_3O_4(s)$$

## Exercise 16

(a) Lead(IV) oxide cannot be made directly by heating lead in oxygen. Dilead(II) lead(IV) oxide (red lead), $Pb_3O_4$, is formed if lead is heated in oxygen at 450 °C. If dilead(II) lead(IV) oxide is treated with dilute nitric acid, lead(IV) oxide is obtained.

(b) Germanium(II) oxide and carbon monoxide.

$$GeO_2(s) + Ge(s) \rightleftharpoons 2GeO(s)$$

$$CO_2(g) + C(s) \rightarrow 2CO(g)$$

(c) Tin(II) oxide and lead(II) oxide.

$$2Sn(NO_3)_2(s) \rightarrow 2SnO(s) + 4NO_2(g) + O_2(g)$$
(SnO is readily oxidized to $SnO_2$ by warming in air)
$$2Pb(NO_3)_2(s) \rightarrow 2PbO(s) + 4NO_2(g) + O_2(g)$$

## Exercise 17

(a) Carbon monoxide can be produced by the incomplete combustion of carbon.

$$2C(s) + O_2(g) \rightarrow 2CO(g)$$

A more efficient method is to pass oxygen through a long combustion tube containing heated carbon. The resulting gas can be passed through sodium hydroxide solution to remove any carbon dioxide formed initially and not reduced by carbon.

$$CO_2(g) + C(s) \rightarrow 2CO(g)$$

(b) If lead is heated with a large excess of oxygen in a furnace above 600 °C lead(II) oxide is formed.

$$2Pb(s) + O_2(g) \rightarrow 2PbO(s)$$

---

## Results Table 4

| Test | Tin(IV) oxide | Lead(IV) oxide |
|---|---|---|
| (a) Heat | No change. | Red liquid formed on heating and colourless gas evolved which relit a glowing splint ($O_2$ evolved). Yellow glassy solid remained. |
| (b) Dilute hydrochloric acid | No reaction. | Slow evolution of a gas which bleached damp litmus paper. Characteristic smell of chlorine detectable. |
| (c) Concentrated hydrochloric acid | No apparent reaction. | Vigorous reaction, chlorine evolved, yellow clear liquid remained with a white solid at the bottom of the test-tube. |
| (d) Concentrated sodium hydroxide | A very small quantity probably dissolved but this was not obvious. | A very small quantity dissolved leaving a brown coloured solution. (This may be $PbO_2$ in suspension.) |
| (e) Acidified potassium iodide | No reaction. | Brown solution formed. |

## Experiment 2. Questions

1. $2PbO_2(s) \rightarrow 2PbO(s) + O_2(g)$.

2. (a) $PbO_2$ is oxidizing chloride ions to chlorine.

   $$PbO_2(s) + 4HCl(aq) \rightarrow PbCl_2(s) + 2H_2O(l) + Cl_2(g)$$

   (b) $PbO_2$ is oxidizing iodide ions to iodine, which dissolves in excess iodide ions.

   $$I_2(s) + I^-(aq) \rightleftharpoons I_3^-(aq)$$

3. The yellow liquid contains the complex ion $[PbCl_6]^{2-}$ (hexachloro-plumbate(IV) ion).

4. (a) $SnO_2(s) + 2OH^-(aq) + 2H_2O(l) \rightarrow [Sn(OH)_6]^{2-}(aq)$
   (b) $PbO_2(s) + 2OH^-(aq) + 2H_2O(l) \rightarrow [Pb(OH)_6]^{2-}(aq)$

5. Both oxides ($SnO_2$ and $PbO_2$) are amphoteric since they react with acids and alkalis.

6. Oxygen will be evolved when red lead is heated:

   $$2Pb_3O_4(s) \rightarrow 6PbO(s) + O_2(g)$$

   This reaction can be regarded as the decomposition of the lead(IV) oxide component of red lead i.e. $2PbO_2(s) \rightarrow 2PbO(s) + O_2(g)$

Table 11

| Formula | Appearance | Bonding and structure | Acid-base nature | Effect of heat* | Formula | Appearance | Bonding and structure | Acid-base nature | Effect of heat* |
|---|---|---|---|---|---|---|---|---|---|
| CO | Colourless gas | Covalent, simple molecular | Neutral | Oxidized on heating | CO₂ | Colourless gas | Covalent, simple molecular | Acidic | Stable even at high temperatures |
| SiO | This solid is very unstable and not well studied. It disproportionates at room temperature forming SiO₂ and Si. Believed to be giant molecular. | | | | SiO₂ | White solid | Covalent, giant molecular. | Acidic | Stable even at high temperatures |
| GeO | Black solid | Mainly ionic Giant ionic. | Amphoteric (mainly acidic) | Oxidized to GeO₂ even on standing in air | GeO₂ | White solid | Intermediate between giant molecular and ionic. Ionic character increases from GeO₂ to PbO₂ | Mainly acidic (amphoteric tendencies) | Stable even at high temperatures |
| SnO | Dark grey solid | Mainly ionic Giant ionic | Amphoteric | Slowly oxidized to SnO₂ on standing in air | SnO₂ | White solid | | Amphoteric (mainly acidic) | Stable even at high temperatures |
| PbO | Normally a yellow solid but a red-yellow solid can also be formed | Mainly ionic Giant ionic | Amphoteric (mainly basic) | Stable even at high temperatures | PbO₂ | Brown solid | | Amphoteric | Decomposes on heating over 300 °C |

*The oxides are heated in air or oxygen.

Exercise 18

(a) Table 11: see opposite.

(b) The stability of the +4 oxides decreases down the group whereas the stability of the +2 oxides increases. These trends agree with the patterns observed in earlier exercises.

(c) As ionic character increases and covalent character decreases so acid-base nature changes from acidic to basic, via the amphoteric stage.

(d) This is true of Group IV, e.g. tin(IV) oxide is more covalent and more acidic than tin(II) oxide.

(e) $SiO_2(s) + 2OH^- \rightarrow SiO_3^{2-} + H_2O(l)$ (fused alkali must be used in this silicate reaction)

$SnO_2(s) + 2OH^-(aq) \rightarrow SnO_3^{2-}(aq) + H_2O(l)$ (or $SnO_2(s) + 2OH^-(aq) + 2H_2O(l) \rightarrow Sn(OH)_6^{2-}(aq)$) stannate(IV)

$PbO_2(s) + 2OH^-(aq) \rightarrow PbO_3^{2-}(aq) + H_2O(l)$ (or $PbO_2(s) + 2OH^-(aq) + 2H_2O(l) \rightarrow Pb(OH)_6^{2-}(aq)$) plumbate(IV)

(f) Germanium(IV) oxide would be expected to react similarly to form germanate(IV) ions, $GeO_3^{2-}$.

Exercise 19

(a) (i) Four C–O bonds are broken in the hypothetical polymer and two C=O bonds are formed in the carbon dioxide molecule.

(ii) Enthalpy change = $[(4 \times 358) - (2 \times 803)]$ kJ mol⁻¹

Enthalpy change = $(+1432 - 1606)$ kJ mol⁻¹

Enthalpy change = $-174$ kJ mol⁻¹

(Note that this enthalpy change is negative because the C=O bond is more than twice as strong as the C–O bond.)

(iii) This value indicates that the reaction goes to the right, and that carbon dioxide exists as single covalent molecules.

(b) Si=O bonds are not known in any compounds so a value cannot be assigned to this bond energy. It is therefore not surprising that discrete molecules of silicon(IV) oxide do not exist since such molecules could contain Si=O bonds. Presumably, Si=O bonds would be less than twice as strong as Si–O bonds and this would make the enthalpy change for the hypothetical change positive.

Exercise 20

(a) Silicon(IV) oxide.

(b) The high stability and high value of $\Delta H_f^{\ominus}$ is due to (i) the relatively low enthalpy of atomization of silicon, which is a consequence of the weak Si–Si bond in the element; (ii) the relatively strong Si–O bond.

(e) See diagram (a) below.

(f) The solvent will gradually change from violet to colourless as the iodine is used up.

(g) See diagram (b) below.

During filtration the solvent and filter funnel will cool down and some tin(IV) iodide is likely to crystallize inside the funnel. Pouring more hot solvent into the funnel will redissolve any crystallized tin(IV) iodide.

(h) Cool the liquid in a refrigerator or allow some of the solvent to evaporate in the fume cupboard.

(i) See diagram (c) below.

Heat the paraffin oil slowly, with continual stirring, and note the temperature at which the solid melts.

(j) The tin(IV) iodide molecules are covalent and tetrahedral.

The orange colour is unusual for the halides in Group IV and indeed uncommon for compounds other than transition metal compounds.

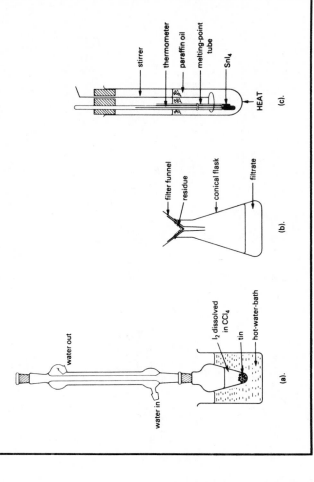

(a).  (b).  (c).

---

Exercise 21

(a) Table 13

| Formula of halide | Appearance at r.t.p.* | Method of preparation | Equation for preparation |
|---|---|---|---|
| $CCl_4$** | Colourless liquid | Pass chlorine through boiling $CS_2$ | $CS_2(l) + 3Cl_2(g) \rightarrow CCl_4(l) + S_2Cl_2(l)$ |
| $SiCl_4$** | Fuming colourless liquid | Pass $Cl_2$ over heated Si | $Si(s) + 2Cl_2(g) \rightarrow SiCl_4(l)$ |
| $GeCl_2$ | Colourless solid | Pass $GeCl_4$ vapour over warm germanium | $GeCl_4(g) + Ge(s) \rightarrow 2GeCl_2(s)$  $GeCl_2$ disproportionates at 75 °C |
| $GeCl_4$ | Fuming colourless liquid | Pass $Cl_2$ over heated Ge | $Ge(s) + 2Cl_2(g) \rightarrow GeCl_4(l)$ |
| $SnCl_2$ | Colourless solid | Pass HCl (gas) over heated Sn | $Sn(s) + 2HCl(g) \rightarrow SnCl_2(s) + H_2(g)$ |
| $SnCl_4$ | Fuming colourless liquid | Pass $Cl_2$ over hot Sn | $Sn(s) + 2Cl_2(g) \rightarrow SnCl_4(l)$ |
| $PbCl_2$ | White solid | Mix $Pb^{2+}$(aq) and $Cl^-$(aq). Immediate white precipitate. (Or heat elements.) | $Pb^{2+}(aq) + 2Cl^-(aq) \rightarrow PbCl_2(s)$ or $Pb(s) + Cl_2(g) \rightarrow PbCl_2(s)$ |
| $PbCl_4$ | Yellow oily liquid | React $PbO_2$ with cold conc. HCl (0 °C) | $PbO_2(s) + 4HCl(aq) \rightarrow PbCl_4(l) + 2H_2O(l)$ ($PbCl_4$ decomposes when warm) |

*r.t.p. = room temperature and pressure
**The dichlorides of C + Si are not known.

(b) Germanium(II) chloride and tin(II) chloride react with chlorine at 25 °C to form the tetrachlorides.

$$XCl_2(s) + Cl_2(g) \rightarrow XCl_4(l) \quad \text{(where X = Ge or Sn)}$$

Exercise 22

(a) $Sn(s) + 2I_2(\text{in } CCl_4) \rightarrow SnI_4(s)$

(b) $CCl_4$ is used as a convenient solvent for the $I_2$. If solid $I_2$ is heated it sublimes and this would prevent it from reacting with the tin.

(c) Amount of tin $= \dfrac{2 \text{ g}}{119 \text{ g mol}^{-1}} = 0.017$ mol

Amount of $I_2 = \dfrac{6.35 \text{ g}}{254 \text{ g mol}^{-1}} = 0.025$ mol

Since 1 mol of Sn reacts with 2 mol of $I_2$, tin is in excess.

(d) 2 mol of $I_2$ produces 1 mol of $SnI_4$ on reaction with excess Sn.

∴ 0.025 mol of $I_2$ produces $\dfrac{0.025}{2}$ mol of $SnI_4$

Mass of $SnI_4 = \dfrac{0.025}{2}$ mol $\times 627$ g mol$^{-1} = \boxed{7.84 \text{ g}}$

Experiment 3. Specimen results.

Results Table 5. Tests with Q.

| Method | Observation | Inference |
|---|---|---|
| (1) A spatula-ful of the powder was heated in an ignition tube, gently at first and then more strongly. | The red-orange solid initially darkened on heating and a colour-less gas was evolved as the solid melted to a red liquid. On cooling the liquid solidified to a yellow solid. | The red-orange colour of Q suggests that it could be $Pb_3O_4$ and that the resulting yellow solid is PbO. |
| A glowing splint was lowered into the tube. | The splint relit as the solid melted. | $O_2$ produced, probably by the decomposition of $Pb_3O_4$ to leave PbO. |
| (2) About 2 $cm^3$ of dilute nitric acid was added to half a spatula-ful of the powder in a test-tube. The mixture was gently heated. | The orange solid turned to a dark brown solid on heating. The resulting brown solid settled to the bottom on standing with a colourless liquid above it. | The PbO part of $Pb_3O_4$ ($2PbO \cdot PbO_2$) dissolves leaving brown $PbO_2$. |
| (3) The colourless liquid from test 2 was decanted off carefully into a test-tube. | | The colourless liquid is likely to contain $Pb^{2+}$(aq). |
| (a) About 1 $cm^3$ was poured into another test-tube and a few drops of KI solution was added. | A yellow precipitate was formed. | Yellow precipitate of $PbI_2$. |
| (b) NaOH(aq) was added to half the remaining solution from (2), drop by drop initially and then to excess. | White precipitate formed initially but this redissolved on addition of excess NaOH(aq). | White precipitate of $Pb(OH)_2$ formed which dissolved to form plumbate(II) ions. |

Results Table 6. Experiment to test inference.

| Inference | Test and observation | Conclusion |
|---|---|---|
| The resulting solution from test (2) contains $Pb^{2+}$(aq). | A yellow precipitate appeared on adding a few drops of $CrO_4^{2-}$(aq) to the unknown solution. The precipitate turned orange on heating. | Yellow $PbCrO_4$ is formed confirming the presence of $Pb^{2+}$. |

Exercise 23

(a) The thermal stability of the tetrachlorides decreases down the group while the thermal stability of the dichlorides increases down the group.

(b) $SnCl_4(l) \xrightarrow{heat} SnCl_2(s) + Cl_2(g)$
    $PbCl_4(l) \xrightarrow{heat} PbCl_2(s) + Cl_2(g)$.

Exercise 24

(a) The outer valence shell of carbon can accommodate only eight electrons, whereas that of silicon can accommodate eighteen. This is because the five vacant 3d orbitals in silicon can be used for bonding.

The hydrolysis of silicon tetrachloride is rapid because silicon can use a d orbital to form a five-coordinate intermediate. This is formed by the donation of a lone pair of electrons from the oxygen atom (in water) into an empty 3d orbital on silicon. Clearly, the hydrolysis of tetrachloromethane cannot proceed via an intermediate since the d orbitals are not available for bonding.

(b) The probable mechanism for the hydrolysis of silicon tetrachloride is as follows:

The $Si(OH)_4$ is believed to undergo condensation polymerization to form hydrated silica $SiO_2 \cdot xH_2O$.

Exercise 25

(a) $XCl_4 + 2H_2O \rightarrow XO_2 + 4HCl$.

(b) All, except $CCl_4$, react with the moisture in the air forming hydrogen chloride.

## Exercise 26

(a) $SnCl_2(s) + H_2O(l) \rightleftharpoons Sn(OH)Cl(aq) + HCl(aq)$.

(b) The addition of hydrochloric acid forces the above equilibrium to the left and thus reduces hydrolysis.

(c) Partial hydrolysis of the compound occurs on heating.

$SnCl_2:2H_2O(s) \rightarrow Sn(OH)Cl(s) + H_2O(l) + HCl(g)$

(d) $SnCl_2(s) + 2Cl^-(aq) \rightarrow [SnCl_3]^-(aq) + Cl^-(aq) \rightleftharpoons [SnCl_4]^{2-}(aq)$
    from      trichlorostannate(II)        tetrachlorostannate(II)
    conc. HCl      ion                           ion

$PbCl_2(aq) + 2Cl^-(aq) \rightleftharpoons [PbCl_4]^{2-}(aq)$
                  tetrachloroplumbate(II) ion

## Exercise 27

### Table 14

| | Similarities between hydrogen and a periodic group | Differences between hydrogen and a periodic group |
|---|---|---|
| Group I | Has one electron in outer shell. Forms monopositive ions. Forms a monoxide and peroxide. | Is a non-metal. Forms mononegative ions. Forms diatomic molecules. Has a much higher electronegativity and first ionization energy. Unreactive with water. |
| Group IV | Has a half-full outer shell. Forms covalent bonds. Is a non-metal. | Forms diatomic molecules. Oxidation states of H range from -1 to +1 and not -4 to +4. Electronegativity is out of step with group trend. Does not have 4 electrons in its outer shell. |
| Group VII | Forms diatomic molecules, covalent bonds and mononegative ions. Has one electron less than the following noble gas in the Periodic Table. Is a non-metal. | Forms monopositive ions (rare in Group VII). Has a lower electronegativity and electron affinity. Does not have 7 electrons in its outer shell. Is a strong reducing agent. |

## Results Table 7

| Test | Observations | Inferences |
|---|---|---|
| 1. To 1 cm³ of the solution of H add aqueous silver nitrate followed by dilute nitric acid. | White precipitate appeared on adding silver nitrate with no further change on adding nitric acid. | AgCl(s) probably precipitated. The solution of H is likely to contain Cl⁻(aq) ions. |
| 2. To 1 cm³ of the solution of H add aqueous sodium hydroxide until in excess. | White precipitate appeared which dissolved on addition of excess NaOH. | The precipitated hydroxide is amphoteric. Thus, any of the following metal ions could be present: $Pb^{2+}$, $Zn^{2+}$, $Al^{3+}$, $Sb^{3+}$, $Sn^{2+}$ and $Sn^{4+}$. |
| 3. To 1 cm³ of aqueous iron(III) chloride add a few drops of aqueous potassium thiocyanate. To this solution add some of the solution of H. | A red solution appeared on adding potassium thiocyanate to iron(III) chloride. The solution decolorized on addition of H. | This indicates that the $Fe^{3+}$ has been reduced to $Fe^{2+}$ by the solution of H. Therefore H is likely to contain $Sn^{2+}$ since this is readily oxidized to $Sn^{4+}$. |
| 4. To 1 cm³ of aqueous mercury(II) chloride add a little of the solution of H, then excess. | A white precipitate initially formed which darkened to a grey solid on standing. | The white precipitate of $Hg_2Cl_2$ is reduced to mercury by the $Sn^{2+}$. |
| 5. Heat some of I in a pyrex boiling-tube. Allow to cool. Add 8-10 cm³ of dilute nitric acid to the residue and boil the mixture for 1 or 2 minutes. Filter if necessary and use portions of the cool solution for the following tests: | Dark brown solid melted on heating and gave off a colourless gas which relit a glowing splint. On further heating the liquid became red and cooled to a glassy yellow-brown solid. | Oxygen evolved probably from the decomposition of brown $PbO_2$ to yellow PbO. |
| (a) To 1 cm³ of the solution add aqueous sodium hydroxide. | A white precipitate was formed which dissolved on addition of excess NaOH. | Precipitated hydroxide is amphoteric. $Pb(OH)_2$ is probably precipitated which dissolves to give a plumbate(II). |
| (b) To 1 cm³ of the solution add dilute sulphuric acid. | A white precipitate is formed. | $PbSO_4$ probably precipitated. |
| (c) To 1 cm³ of the solution add aqueous potassium chromate(VI). | Yellow precipitate formed. | $PbCrO_4$ precipitated. Confirms the presence of $Pb^{2+}$. |

In the reactions 2 to 4 lead is in the +4 oxidation state. In reactions 3 and 4 it is reduced to its more stable oxidation state of +2.

## Exercise 28

(a) (i)

| | H | Li | F |
|---|---|---|---|
| Atomic (covalent) radius/nm | 0.037 | 0.123 | 0.072 |

Bond dissociation energy of $H_2$ = 436 kJ mol$^{-1}$
Bond dissociation energy of $F_2$ = 158 kJ mol$^{-1}$

(ii) No value is assigned to the ionic radius of the $H^+$ ion because the ion consists of a 'bare' proton.

(b) Since the fluorine atoms are very small the repulsions between the non-bonding electrons on each fluorine atom in the fluorine molecule ($F_2$) significantly weaken the F-F bond. The hydrogen molecule ($H_2$) does not possess non-bonding electrons, so similar repulsions do not arise.

(c) The following factors are responsible for the unique nature of hydrogen:

(i) Its atoms are very small.

(ii) Its positive ion consists of a 'bare' proton.

(iii) Its bond dissociation energy is very high.

(iv) Its half-filled valence shell enables it to form mono-positive and mono-negative ions.

## Exercise 29

(a) Lead-based paints, lead storage tanks and pipes for carrying drinking water and lead in petrol can pollute the environment.

(b) Lead in petrol is chiefly responsible for pollution.

(c) Tetraethyl-lead(IV), $(C_2H_5)_4Pb$, and tetramethyl-lead(IV), $(CH_3)_4Pb$, are added to petrol.

(d) The lead compounds are added to petrol in order to slow down the rate of combustion of the fuel when ignited and thus minimise 'knocking'.

## Exercise 30

(a) Lead can be absorbed from the gut and lungs but absorption is more efficient from the lungs.

(b) (i) Airborne lead and lead in plants are much reduced beyond a distance of about 150 m from the road. This may indicate that people living very near busy roads are at greater risk. Also blood-lead levels are generally higher in inner-city dwellers than in country dwellers. However we all ingest a lot of lead in food and water; although absorption is less effective by this means, the quantity involved is considerable.

(ii) Children are more at risk from lead pollution than adults.

(c) The symptoms of severe lead poisoning are: intestinal spasms, tremors and paralysis, failure of kidney function and convulsions.

(d) By sub-acute lead poisoning the author probably means mild lead poisoning, the symptoms of which are vague. (Strictly speaking the phrase 'sub-acute' refers to the time course of an illness and not its severity.)

(e) The limits of lead are continuously under debate for the following reasons.

(i) It is difficult to decide the limit beyond which lead becomes a danger to health, since the milder symptoms of lead poisoning, such as fatigue, depression and digestive upsets, can occur for many other reasons.

(ii) Economic and political considerations also play an important role. (You might find it useful to discuss these points with other students and teachers.)

## Exercise 31

(a) Lead concentration in the blood is one indicator of sub-acute lead poisoning.
The excretion of δ-aminolaevulinic acid (ALA) is also a sensitive indicator of lead poisoning. This occurs if the enzyme of δ-ALA dehydratase is inhibited by lead.

(b) The measurement of the concentration of lead in the discarded milk-teeth of children.